STORM-333

KGB and Spetsnaz seize Kabul, Soviet–Afghan War 1979

MARK GALEOTTI

OSPREY PUBLISHING
Bloomsbury Publishing Plc
PO Box 883, Oxford, OX1 9PL, UK
1385 Broadway, 5th Floor, New York, NY 10018, USA
E-mail: info@ospreypublishing.com
www.ospreypublishing.com

OSPREY is a trademark of Osprey Publishing Ltd

First published in Great Britain in 2021

A catalogue record for this book is available from the British Library.

ISBN: PB 9781472841872; eBook 9781472841889;
ePDF 9781472841858; XML 9781472841865

21 22 23 24 25   10 9 8 7 6 5 4 3 2 1

Battlescenes by Johnny Shumate
Cover art by Mark Stacey
Maps by www.bounford.com
3D BEV by Alan Gilliland
Index by Alan Rutter
Typeset by PDQ Digital Media Solutions, Bungay, UK
Printed and bound in India by Replika Press Private Ltd.

Author's note

Translating out of Cyrillic always poses challenges. With the exception of
the genitive masculine -ogo ending (that sounds like -ovo), I have generally
chosen to transliterate words as they are pronounced (so, for example, Petr
is rendered as Pyotr). I have also ignored the diacritical 'soft' and 'hard' signs
found in the original.

Cover art

Soviet *Spetsnaz* commandos bail out of their BTR-60PB personnel carrier
under heavy machine gun fire as they approach the Tajbeg Palace. They are
wearing Afghan army uniforms, but with white armbands as a recognition
symbol. Their use of AK-74 rifles rather than the older AK-47 is, however, a
clear sign of their status.

Glossary of terms and acronyms used in this text

APC	Armoured Personnel Carrier
ATGM	Anti-Tank Guided Missile
BG	*Boyevaya Gruppa*: Combat Group
BMD	*Boyevaya Mashina Desanta*: Airborne Combat Vehicle
BMP	*Boyevaya Mashina Pyekhoty*: Infantry Combat Vehicle
BTR	*Bronetransportyor*: Armoured Transporter
BTR-D	*Bronetransportyor Desanta*: Airborne Armoured Transporter
DRA	Democratic Republic of Afghanistan
GRU	*Glavnoye Razvedyvatelnoye Upravleniye*: Main Intelligence Directorate (of the General Staff), military intelligence
IFV	Infantry Fighting Vehicle
KAM	*Kargarano Amniyati Mu'asasa*: Workers' Security Institution (i.e. political police, later renamed State Intelligence Service, KhAD)
KGB	*Komitet Gosudarstvennoi bezopasnosti*: Committee of State Security
KUOS	*Kursy usovershenstvovaniya ofitserskogo sostava*: Officer Development Courses (KGB special operations training programme)
OSN	*Otryad Spetsialnogo Naznacheniya*: Special Purpose Detachment (a *Spetsnaz* unit equivalent to a battalion)
PDPA	People's Democratic Party of Afghanistan
PGU	*Pervoye Glavnoye Upravleniye*: First Chief Directorate (KGB's foreign intelligence arm)
Sarandoy	'Defenders', the PDPA's paramilitary gendarmerie, part of the Interior Ministry
Spetsnaz	*Spetsialnogo Naznacheniya*: Special Purpose, i.e. special forces (literally, Special Designation)
TurkVO	*Turkestansky voyenny okrug*: Turkestan Military District
VDV	*Vozdushno-Desantnye Voiska*: Air Assault Troops (i.e. paratroopers)

CONTENTS

INTRODUCTION

Look after your own property, and you won't accuse your neighbour of being a thief.
Afghan proverb

Storm-333 was the Soviet operation that began its invasion of Afghanistan in December 1979, a decapitating strike to remove existing leader Hafizullah Amin and replace him with Moscow's chosen successor, and also to paralyse the Afghan command system to ensure no resistance. As such, it was in many ways a textbook operation, one that successfully carried out its mission against often fierce resistance, with far fewer casualties than anticipated. The irony is, of course, that this triumph launched a lengthy, misconceived and miserable war that the Soviets did not truly lose – in military terms, at least – but certainly failed to win. What was intended as a six-month stabilization operation ended up becoming a ten-year war that left some 15,000 Soviets and perhaps a million Afghans dead.

Then again, Afghanistan is hardly a stranger to the interference of imperial powers, and Afghans are used to dashing their hopes of quick, neat victory. In 1838, the British invaded to replace Emir Dost Mohammad as ruler in Kabul with his rival Shah Shuja. Later, after the bloody 1842 retreat from Kabul, they had to put Dost Mohammad Khan back into power. In 2001, a US-led invasion toppled the Taliban and placed Hamid Karzai in power – and allied forces are still mired there. In between, it was the Soviet Union's turn to try – and ultimately fail – to impose its will on the recalcitrant Afghans.

After all, the Cold War was a time of coups and killings, of inconvenient regimes being toppled and friendly dictators propped up. Moscow had never really considered Afghanistan – rural, Muslim, fragmented and decentralized – as either a crucial battleground or a likely candidate for Marxism–Leninism. Indeed, the commissars of the Kremlin had had perfectly amicable relations with King Mohammed Zahir Shah, who reigned from 1933 to 1973. As one retired Soviet diplomat of the times told me, essentially 'they didn't bother us, and we didn't bother them'. The Soviets were happy to provide development aid while asking or expecting little in return. A bloodless coup in 1973 by Mohammed Daoud Khan – who had been at once the king's cousin, brother-in-law and prime minister in a triumph of multi-tasking – meant that a monarchy became a republic, but also brought a more forceful policy towards Afghanistan's place in the world that, as discussed below, led to the eventual Soviet intervention.

In many ways, this reflected the assumptions of the times – and the specific blind spots of the leaders in Moscow. Although one can question how far they really believed in their Marxist–Leninist ideology, as they enjoyed the privileged lifestyle of the Party's *nomenklatura* elite and watched corruption and black marketeering hollow out the planned economy, they certainly all bought into the notion that the USSR and the USA were locked in a zero-sum contest for the globe. By definition, a country 'lost' from the Soviet sphere of influence was 'gained' by the Americans, and vice versa. Furthermore, they were scared that they were falling behind: politically, economically, technologically. The era of the computer was really just beginning, and the Soviets were painfully aware of just how far behind the West they were. The economy was stagnating, and the population was becoming restive, whatever lies the clumsy official propaganda tried to tell them. In this environment, the old men running the country – General Secretary Leonid Brezhnev was 72, and by the time of his death in 1982, the median age of the ruling Politburo, in effect the cabinet, was 70 – feared that to show any signs of weakness might only encourage more pressure from both outside and inside their borders.

Where did they still feel strong? In the power and discipline of their intelligence and security service, the KGB, and their military. In this time of decay and decline, increasingly they would turn to them as their instruments of last resort, as the Afghans would discover in 1979.

This imposing memorial for fallen special operations soldiers of recent Soviet and Russian wars in the Moscow suburb of Khimki cites both *Zenit* and *Grom* along with more regular *Spetsnaz* units. (Andrei Subbotin/CC 3.0)

Afghanistan has certainly earned its title as the 'Graveyard of Empires', through the centuries. William Barnes Wollen's 'The Last Stand of the 44th Regiment at Gundamuck' captures the last battle of the disastrous British retreat from Kabul in 1842, which left only one survivor. (DeAgostini/Getty Images)

ORIGINS

If the revolution is successful, we will get a lasting headache.

Colonel General Sergei Akhromeyev, 1978

Daoud had seized power thanks to the support of key figures within the military, including Chief of Staff General Abdul Karim Mustaghni, as well as the *Parcham* wing of the Marxist People's Democratic Party of Afghanistan (PDPA). It was an easy transition of power, because King Zahir Shah – who had been undergoing medical treatment in Italy – opted to abdicate and stay in agreeable exile in a villa outside Rome. It was also easy because while the government in Kabul might have all the trappings of power, especially in the country's towns and cities, its real authority in the countryside was rather minimal.

However, Daoud had ambitions. He hailed from the country's Pashtun majority and was a forceful advocate of creating a larger 'Pashtunistan', uniting parts of Afghanistan and Pakistan. He also wanted to reshape the country, and although he initially promised 'genuine democracy' he moved quickly to consolidate his personal power, disbanding the existing parliament and pushing through a new constitution creating a presidential one-party state. However, it was easier to claim power than to assert it, and his clumsy efforts at modernization at home and pushing his Pashtun agenda abroad soon generated resistance from every quarter.

Daoud actively sought Soviet assistance, but the irony is that this only made Moscow begin to pay more attention to Afghanistan, and expect

The day after the *Saur* Revolution, soldiers contemplate a burned-out Afghan army BMP in Kabul. *Khalq*'s success in penetrating the Afghan officer corps ensured that it was able to seize power relatively quickly, although not without some serious fighting. (Cleric77/CC 3.0)

a return on its investment. For years, Kabul had been at once formally non-aligned, yet the recipient of extensive Soviet support, from hand-me-down weapons to economic assistance. The Kremlin began pushing its own interests – especially as regarded Afghanistan's policies towards Pakistan – and Daoud began to find that irksome. To quote the same diplomat as before, who had met Daoud in 1977, 'he didn't seem to realize that the more he asked from us, the more we expected from him'.

Meanwhile, Daoud's erstwhile allies in the PDPA were becoming disillusioned. Formed in 1965, it was essentially a party of the urban, educated elites and junior army officers, although it was split between the *Khalq* ('Masses') and *Parcham* ('Banner') factions. *Parcham* largely advocated a slower move towards socialism, and drew its support mainly from the urban, educated elites, while *Khalq* was more radical, more impatient, and was primarily based in the Pashtun population, especially poorer and less-educated classes. *Parcham* had supported Daoud's coup, while *Khalq* refused to cooperate with him and instead actively worked to build up its supporters – especially

The formal public portrait of Hafizullah Amin, who seized power in 1979 by the simple expedient of having his predecessor strangled. (Wikimedia Common/Public Domain)

within the military. The Soviets tried to get the two factions to reconcile with each other, and in 1977, *Parcham*'s Babrak Karmal and *Khalq*'s Nur Mohammed Taraki and Hafizullah Amin formally agreed to work together, but this was always a deeply embittered movement.

Daoud had become increasingly worried about the PDPA. In April 1978, Mir Akbar Khyber, a high-profile member of *Parcham*, was assassinated. Although it may well have been Amin who was actually behind it, at the time the assumption was that it was the government. Some 15,000 people rallied at his funeral, and Daoud panicked, ordering a round-up of PDPA leaders. In response, on 27–28 April 1978, the PDPA launched a coup of its own. *Khalq* by this time had a powerful network within the military, and a tank column shelled and took the presidential palace, while fighters from the air force hit it with rockets. Daoud was killed in this so-called '*Saur* Revolution' ('April Revolution') and a new, revolutionary regime established.

This Democratic Republic of Afghanistan (DRA) was run by Taraki, as Chairman of the Revolutionary Council, Karmal as First Deputy Prime Minister, and Hafizullah Amin as Foreign Minister. What was clearly an attempt to show unity within the PDPA soon foundered, though. In July 1979, Karmal was sent into effective exile as ambassador to Czechoslovakia and all other *Parchamis* in senior positions were sacked and demoted. Even this proved insufficient: in August, Taraki and Amin used a spurious plot to execute and arrest a series of real or potential rivals. The cannibalistic frenzy continued: next month, Amin deposed Taraki and later had his bodyguard strangle Afghanistan's self-proclaimed 'Great Teacher'.

HAFIZULLAH AMIN

Hafizullah Amin has been described as a radical Marxist, a born schemer and an ardent modernizer, but ultimately he proved to be a man driven more than anything else by the need for power and a belief that ruthlessness and determination could sweep aside any obstacles in his way. The view of many Soviet officials who worked with him, after all, was that he claimed to be a Marxist because he was struggling against a conservative order, but defeating his enemies mattered more to him than what he could do with that victory. Born in 1929 to a minor Gilzai Pashtun civil service family, he was lucky to get the schooling to be able to enter Kabul University to read mathematics, going on to become a schoolteacher. In 1957, he went to study at Columbia University in New York, and there he became influenced by Marxism and the rising anti-colonial movement of the time. He returned to Afghanistan and became increasingly interested in politics, also coming to know the Afghan communist Nur Mohammed Taraki, with whom he would later form an alliance. After a second time in the USA, at the University of Wisconsin, Amin ditched his doctoral studies for full-time politics. In elections in 1965, he ran as a candidate for the PDPA, losing by a margin of fewer than 50 votes. Nonetheless, he was elected a candidate (non-voting) member of the PDPA's Central Committee, and when the party split between *Khalq* and *Parcham* in 1967, he joined the former. In 1969, he was the only member of *Khalq* elected to parliament. (Babrak Karmal was the only member of *Parcham* elected, and it was observed that Amin treated Karmal worse than even the most conservative, anti-communist parliamentarians.)

When the republic was created by Daoud's 1973 coup, the *Khalq* goal was to undermine it. Amin swiftly became second only to Taraki in the movement, providing the ruthlessness and tactical skills to complement Taraki's personal authority. Amin's efforts focused on winning support for *Khalq* within the armed forces, and this allowed the PDPA – which had formally reunited in 1977, although there was still much bad blood between the factions – to stage the *Saur* Revolution in 1978.

In the new regime, Amin moved quickly and effectively to raise his own status and also to marginalize *Parcham*. He also pushed for a maximalist political and economic programme, both because he felt that conservative resistance in the country needed to be broken by an all-out assault rather than incremental reform, and also because this gave him the opportunity to raise his own status by articulating a clear and dramatic message. As Taraki vacillated, urged by both Soviet ambassador Puzanov and other leading PDPA members to sack or demote his former right-hand man, it was Amin who struck first. In September 1979, Amin removed Taraki in a coup.

There is no doubt that Amin was able, intelligent and energetic. However, he was also obsessed with personal power, suspicious of those around him and often resistant to the least compromises. This made him almost as dangerous a friend as an enemy, and led to his eventual downfall.

Moscow had been observing all this with considerable dismay. It had been perfectly comfortable with the king; it had been willing to haggle with

Daoud; now it was having to deal with a regime that was ostensibly committed to the same ideology but which appeared dangerously unstable. This was why Colonel General Akhromeyev, one of the sharpest minds of his generation, had expressed his concerns when news broke of the *Saur* Revolution. Of course, in public, Moscow could only welcome and recognize this new Marxist–Leninist nation, but in private it was doing everything it could to counsel unity and caution.

To no avail. Having driven *Parcham* out of government, Amin was not going

Afghan tank crews scramble to their T-55s. Although their uniforms are virtually indistinguishable here from Soviet ones, especially the distinctive ribbed soft helmets, note the DRA emblem on the side of the turret. (Russian Ministry of Defence/CC 4.0)

to let them back in. Furthermore, he was determined to push ahead with a radical programme that was poorly thought-through and often explicitly aimed at the country's Islamic traditions and existing social structures. It was inevitably going to create massive resistance in the traditional countryside, with land reform perceived as virtual nationalization, while a ban on existing (admittedly usurious) rural credit with no alternatives in place led to an agrarian crisis. Protests were met with repression, and the KAM secret police began rounding up more and more people, from village elders to mullahs: in just over a year, possibly as many as 7,000 people were executed in the infamous Pul-i-Charkhi prison to the east of Kabul.

Afghans are not known for taking such insults lightly. By the end of 1978, tribal revolts and acts of individual resistance were on the rise. The informal social contract of the country had always been that Kabul was welcome to pretend to run the country, so long as it didn't actually try to make good on that claim. Now that it was, and in a way that seemed to run up against every custom and practice of rural society, the country fought back. In October 1978, mass risings took place in the eastern Kunar Valley

Afghan rebels near the burned-out shell of a DRA BTR-60PAI personnel carrier, an earlier version of the ubiquitous BTR-60PB, another example of the dated Soviet equipment used by the Afghans. (Getty Images)

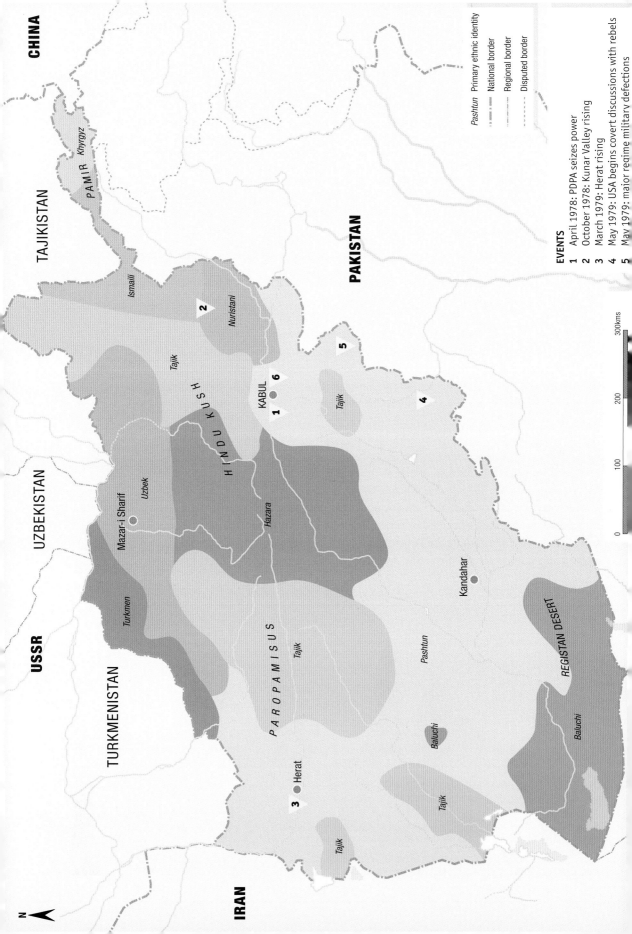

CHINA

TAJIKISTAN

UZBEKISTAN

USSR

TURKMENISTAN

IRAN

PAKISTAN

Khyrgyz

PAMIR

Ismaili

Nuristani

Tajik

2

H I N D U   K U S H

Uzbek

Mazar-i Sharif

Tajik

6
KABUL
1

Tajik

5

Tajik

4

Hazara

P A R O P A M I S U S

Tajik

Pashtun

Kandahar

Baluchi

REGISTAN DESERT

Tajik

3 Herat

Baluchi

N

0	100	200	300kms

EVENTS

Pashtun   Primary ethnic identity

National border

Regional border

Disputed border

1   April 1978: PDPA seizes power
2   October 1978: Kunar Valley rising
3   March 1979: Herat rising
4   May 1979: USA begins covert discussions with rebels
5   May 1979: major regime military defections

THE HERAT RISING

On 15 March 1979, protesters assembled at village mosques and then marched on the city. They were soon joined by thousands of townspeople, who began attacking government buildings and defacing government symbols and posters. The DRA's 17th Division, based in Herat, was called out to suppress the riots, but instead it mutinied. Some soldiers simply deserted, others joined the protesters. For a week, the city was in rebel hands, and gangs of insurgents roamed the streets, looting the bazaar and hunting down officials and those deemed aligned with the regime, especially teachers. Several Soviet civilian advisers and their families were lynched, and according to some reports their bodies dragged round the city.

The authorities initially refused to believe the scale of the disaster, but then responded with ruthless decision. The city was bombed from the air and attacked from the ground, as an armoured column from Kandahar was then reinforced by two tank brigades from Kabul region. By the time the city had been recaptured – and KAM security troops and the *Sarandoy* paramilitary police had finished their arrests and reprisal killings – the death toll had been estimated at anything from 3,000 to a rather implausible 25,000.

Every bit as important were the political consequences. The rebellion acquired a new momentum. Taraki began to wonder if Amin had pushed him into too radical a programme, opening the split that would lead to his murder. The DRA increased its requests for Soviet military assistance. And the old men in Moscow began to wonder just what sort of a problem was emerging on their southern border, and what they might have to do about it.

Mujahideen in Kunar, one of the cradles of their insurrection. The rebels at this stage lacked modern weapons or foreign backers, but they had local support and knowledge and considerably greater enthusiasm than most government troops sent against them. (Erwin Lux/CC-SA 3.0)

region, with bands of *mujahideen*, 'holy warriors', joining with mutineers from the army's 38th Brigade to create a virtual rebel fiefdom. However, one of the most pivotal events took place to the west in Herat. In March 1979, it fell to a spontaneous rebellion which saw Soviet civilians butchered, the DRA's 17th Division mutiny and the country's third city held by protesters for a week.

Taraki began urgently requesting Soviet assistance to crush the rebellion because he could not rely on the military. The Kremlin was willing to send more materiel, including T-62 tanks and Mi-24 helicopter gunships, as well as expanding the force of some 2,000 military advisers already there. However, it refused to send combat troops, telling Taraki that this would only exacerbate protest in the country. Meanwhile, the Soviets were becoming increasingly disenchanted with the *Khalqis*, whom they considered dangerous

extremists. Chairman of the Council of Ministers Alexei Kosygin, warned that 'Amin and Taraki alike are concealing the true state of affairs from us'.

The situation continued to worsen, with army units increasingly mutinying, defecting to the rebels or simply evaporating through widespread desertion. Garrisons in Jalalabad, Ghazni, Nahrin, and even Kabul's Bala Hissar fort mutinied, and while all were suppressed, they conveyed a sense that the regime was simply unable to deal with the threat. By the end of 1979, a 100,000-strong military had shrunk to around 60,000 men, and, if anything, the situation worsened once Amin had replaced Taraki.

By winter 1979, the rebel *mujahideen* numbered some 40,000 men, and were active in 16 of the country's 27 provinces. Kunar, Laghman, Paktia and Paktika provinces were almost wholly under their control, and in 12 more – Badakhshan, Badghis, Farah, Ghazni, Ghowr, Helmand, Herat, Jowzjan, Kapisa, Logar, Takhar and Zabol – the government presence was confined to the main cities. Only three provinces, Baghlan, Kabul and Kunduz, were fully under the PDPA's control.

As if this were not bad enough, in October Amin – who spoke good English and had studied at Columbia University in New York – reached out to the Americans. Until then, he had had only the most cursory of contacts

UNRELIABLE INTEL?

There is now a wealth of Soviet documentation available on discussions around what to do with Afghanistan and the PDPA, but one question which has still not been truly cleared up relates to how far Moscow was being fed biased reports from its agents on the spot. The Soviet ambassador in Kabul until the start of November 1979, Alexander Puzanov, was a veteran to say the least – he was 73 at the time – and according to a number of accounts had a good personal relationship with Taraki. He was genuinely shocked by Amin's treatment of his erstwhile patron, and this undoubtedly coloured his reporting on the situation.

Even more interesting is the role of Lieutenant General Boris Ivanov, the KGB's *rezident* or head of station in Kabul. He consistently lobbied for Soviet forces to be deployed, warning first that the PDPA might be replaced with a hostile Islamist government, along the lines of the recent Iranian revolution, and then that Amin was a closet CIA agent. Interestingly enough, this actually went against the instincts of his boss, KGB chief Yuri Andropov, who ultimately backed intervention but had been deeply sceptical about the move. Ivanov's reporting may have reflected his genuine belief, but it likely was also an attempt to hype Kabul's position as a front line in the Cold War. After all, a posting to Kabul was no plum job, and his career seemed in the doldrums. Making more of the situation – and his reporting certainly influenced Brezhnev – might have seemed a good way to get his career moving. In a way, that was true. Andropov, notoriously committed to getting true and accurate data, removed him from field work in 1980, as no evidence of any CIA connection emerged, although he remained a foreign affairs adviser to the Party.

with them, but he met with Archer Blood of the US mission in Kabul. The meeting was lengthy, friendly, and at once secret and highly public: few details were given of what was discussed, but it led the news on Afghan TV. It is unclear quite what Amin was after – was he trying to avoid excessive dependence on Moscow, or simply wanting to ensure that the Americans did not support the rebellion? – but this was almost guaranteed to stoke Moscow's paranoias. This was especially the case given how Taraki's murder had shocked Brezhnev, who had personally endorsed him ('What scum Amin is,' he reportedly said, 'you smother a man with whom you participated in a revolution'), as well as Alexander Puzanov, the Soviet ambassador to Kabul at the time, who pushed the narrative that Amin might be threatening to double-cross Moscow.

Encouraged by ominous reporting from their people in Kabul, the Soviet leadership, which had hitherto considered Afghanistan no more than an irritation, suddenly began to consider Amin a threat. In 1972, the Egyptian leader Anwar Sadat had expelled his Soviet advisers and sided instead with the Americans. Might Amin be planning the same? If he turned to Washington, the thinking ran, the USA would have an outpost right on the Soviet borders, a base for listening stations and even missiles. When the DRA appealed for military assistance in the spring, after the Herat rising, the deliberations had been careful and cautious, leaning heavily on the opinion of Soviet military specialists. Suddenly, the approach shifted and the real debate was being had by just five men: Brezhnev, KGB head Yuri Andropov, Foreign Minister Andrei Gromyko, Defence Minister Dmitry Ustinov, and Mikhail Suslov, the Party's chief ideologist.

On 4 December, a secret delegation flew to Kabul from Moscow's Chkalovsky airbase. It was headed by the KGB's Lieutenant General Vadim Kirpichenko, a veteran intelligence officer (who, just in case, carried a diplomatic passport identifying him as one 'Pyotr Nikolayev') and a team of officers from the VDV (Air Assault Forces) Operations Group under Lieutenant General Nikolai Guskov, deputy commander of the VDV. Andropov had tasked Kirpichenko with assessing the situation on the ground and developing the broad outlines of a plan to stabilize the country. His first meeting in Kabul was with the KGB *rezident*, Lieutenant General Ivanov, and Chief Soviet Military Adviser General Sultan Magometov, and at an early point it became clear there was no consensus in-country about quite what to do.

In short order, though, the decision was made to remove Amin and replace him with a more moderate and tractable figure, Babrak Karmal, and for what was expected to be a brief, limited military deployment to calm the country down. It was not to prove one of the Soviets' best ideas.

Yuri Andropov, head of the KGB, played a complex and crucial role in the decision-making over Afghanistan. By instinct he was opposed to invasion, but he was convinced by reports of rising instability and Amin's talks with the Americans – and also eager not to appear weak, as he was preparing for a bid to succeed Leonid Brezhnev as General Secretary. (Author's Collection)

INITIAL STRATEGY

The decision has been made to deploy several contingents of Soviet troops in southern regions of the country to the territory of the Democratic Republic of Afghanistan in order to provide international aid to the friendly Afghan people and also to create favourable conditions to interdict possible anti-Afghan actions from neighbouring countries.

Soviet Defence Ministry Directive No. 312/12/001 of 24 December 1979

Although Amin had been begging for Soviet troops to support his regime, from the Kremlin's point of view he was the main problem: his brutal purges of the PDPA were wiping out the cadres needed to maintain the regime and hollowing out the military, his heavy-handed and counter-productive modernization campaign was setting the country ablaze, and his overtures to Washington raised the prospect of Afghanistan changing its allegiance. Ultimately, though, their belief was that the PDPA was fundamentally healthy and that a more moderate and conciliatory leader and a more sensitive and gradualist policy would be able to turn things around. The goals of the intervention were thus three: to remove Amin and replace him with *Parcham*'s Babrak Karmal; to seize the country rapidly enough that the DRA's military would not be forced to choose between resistance and surrender, so that it could be preserved to fight the *mujahideen*; and to make a quick, convincing show of force to cow the rebellion.

From the first, this was a strategy based on dubious assumptions and a great deal of over-optimism. The military High Command was very unhappy at the idea, not least feeling that the proposed deployment of 75,000–80,000 troops was too many for a surgical strike, too few for a comprehensive pacification of the country. This was in many ways a clumsy compromise from the 35,000–40,000 the KGB thought would be enough (this had been Kirpichenko's estimate) and the kind of overwhelming force the military preferred. It was, after all, proportionally smaller in terms of the ratio of troops to area or troops to population than the eventual – and unsuccessful

– US force in Vietnam. It was also only a fraction of the quarter of a million troops used in 1968 to crush the liberal 'Prague Spring', despite the fact that Czechoslovakia was much more politically and geographically propitious for such an operation.

Nonetheless, this was a political decision, and preparations began on 10 December. Ustinov gave Ogarkov verbal orders to set up a new Combined Arms Army in TurkVO (the Turkestan Military District, which bordered Afghanistan), and to prepare an airborne division, an independent airborne regiment, and five Military Transport Aviation divisions for an airlift, while two divisions in the TurkVO were to be brought to combat readiness and reinforced with a pontoon bridge regiment from the Kiev Military District.

On 12 December, the Politburo approved without debate a very bland resolution 'Concerning The Situation In "A"' that didn't even mention Afghanistan by name or invasion in any way, and which was nonetheless so secret that it had been handwritten by Brezhnev's understudy Konstantin Chernenko, so that even Kremlin typists would not get to see it. This one-page document nonetheless set the whole operation in motion:

Defence minister Marshal Dmitry Ustinov (centre) posing with his Chief of the General Staff Nikolai Ogarkov (far left) amidst airborne troopers during the Zapad-81 exercises. For all his medals and uniform, Ustinov was not a soldier and would often have turbulent relationships with his high command, especially the forceful Ogarkov. (US DIA/Public Domain)

> Top Secret
>
> Chaired by Comrade L. I. Brezhnev
>
> Also present: Suslov M. A., Grishin V. V., Kirilenko A. P., Pelshe A. Ya., Ustinov D. F., Chernenko K. U., Andropov Yu. V., Gromyko A. A., Tikhonov N. A., Ponomaryov B. N.
>
> Resolution of the Communist Party Central Committee
>
> Concerning the Situation in 'A'
>
> 1. To ratify the evaluations and measures set forth by Andropov Yu. V., Ustinov D. E., and Gromyko A. A. authorize them to introduce amendments of a non-essential character in the course of the execution of these measures.
>
> Questions requiring the decision of the Central Committee should be expeditiously introduced to the Politburo.
>
> The execution of all these measures should be entrusted to Comrades Andropov Yu. V., Ustinov D. F., and Gromyko A. A.
>
> 2. To entrust Comrades Andropov Yu. V., Ustinov D. E. and Gromyko A. A. to keep the CC Politburo informed on the status of the execution of the measures outlined.
>
> Secretary of the Central Committee Brezhnev
>
> No. 997-[0p] (l p) Protocol 176/125 of 12/12

Baikal-79

The main invasion itself, codenamed Baikal-79, is beyond the scope of this book[1] but essentially combined the airlift of a reinforced paratrooper division directly into Kabul, while ground forces crossed the border at Kushka to

1   See Gregory Fremont-Barnes, *The Soviet–Afghan War 1979–89*, Osprey Essential Histories 75

OGARKOV VS USTINOV

Defence Minister Ustinov may have held the rank of Marshal of the Soviet Union and loved parading in a uniform liberally crusted with medals, but he had never been a soldier. Instead, 'Uncle Mitya' had since the Second World War been a defence industry manager, and while his efforts to ensure the armaments factories kept running in the face of the Axis onslaught were impressive and crucial, it meant he never truly had the respect of the General Staff, nor a real understanding of their concerns. He was hard-working and efficient, but also one of Brezhnev's drinking cronies, with a reputation for never contradicting or disappointing the boss. This was evident in the discussions about intervention into Afghanistan. Ustinov's instincts were that the Soviet Union needed to demonstrate its strength, and that there was no problem that could not be solved by the Red Army. At least as importantly, he was a constant lobbyist for increased defence spending, and he could not afford to admit, in essence, that for all the billions of rubles spent on the military, they were unable to deal with Amin.

His Chief of the General Staff, Nikolai Ogarkov, was a brilliant but abrasive man, and made no secret of his views about intervention. He mistrusted Ustinov anyway as a representative of the so-called 'metal-eaters' of the defence industrial complex, and he and his team (including the aforementioned Akhromeyev) were painfully aware that an army built for mass mechanized war on the plains of Europe was not best suited for a messy counter-insurgency conflict in a mountainous Islamic nation.

Alexander Liakhovsky, the Russian military scholar who has arguably done the most to unearth the behind-the-scenes details of the process, relates the experiences of General Valentin Varennikov, then head of the General Staff's Main Operations Directorate. He recounted how, after various more indirect efforts to change his mind:

'Ogarkov made a last attempt to convince Minister of Defence D. F. Ustinov not to do it. ... [He] invited S. F. Akhromeyev and myself and informed us that he would like, in our presence, to state the inexpediency of such a move... When we came to Ustinov's office, he was with the head of the Main Political Directorate A. A. Yepishev. Nikolai Vasilyevich [Ogarkov] presented for a long time, trying to substantiate the inexpediency of such a move and to convince Ustinov of this. At the end of Ogarkov's presentation the minister did not comment, but only asked Yepishev, "Aleksei Alekseyevich, do you have any questions?" The head of the MPD responded: "No I have no questions. The General Staff always have their own special opinion." Ustinov said: "This is true. But I will take the opinion of the General Staff into account."'

Maybe he did, but ultimately, politics trumped professionalism and Ustinov made no moves to oppose the invasion. Although Ogarkov faithfully followed orders and played a key role in the preparations for the operation, on 10 December he made a last-ditch effort to avert it, warning a Politburo meeting that 'We will re-establish the entire eastern Islamic system against us and we will lose politically in the entire world.' Andropov sharply rebuked him: 'Stick to military affairs! We, the Party, and Leonid Ilyich [Brezhnev] will handle policy!'

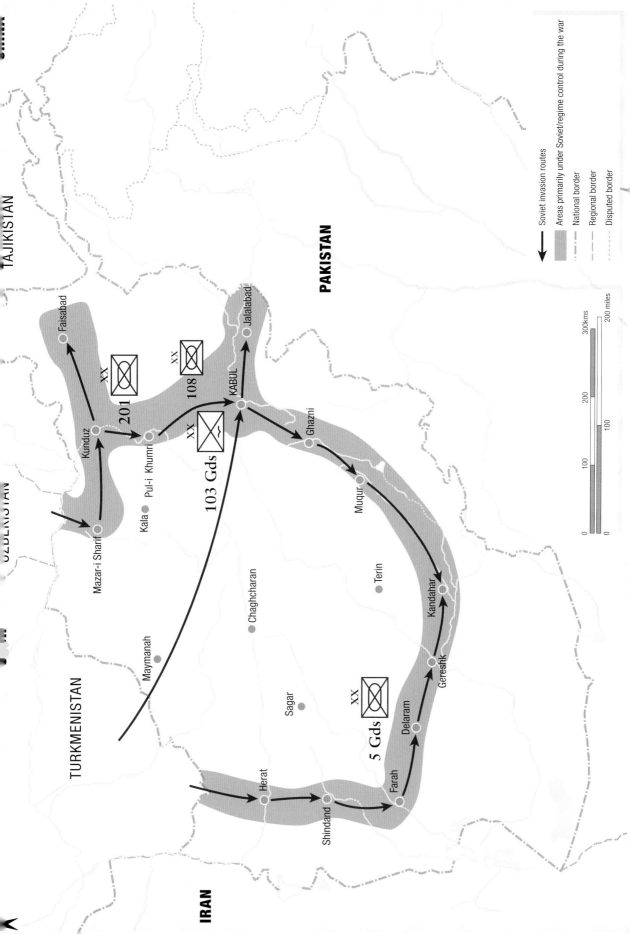

A line-up of aircraft from the DRA's 366th Fighter Regiment at Kandahar, a unit that performed well in the coming war, even if its MiG-17 fighter jets, first deployed in 1952, were essentially interceptors, with rather less value in ground attack. (Georgy Nadezhdin/ TASS via Getty Images)

the north-west and Termez to the north-east and swung round the main ring road connecting the country's principal cities. The main goals were the population centres: this was essentially seen as a show of force rather than a village-by-village pacification mission. The expectation was that most Soviet forces would remain in-country only perhaps six months, and DRA forces, freed from the need to garrison the cities, would take on the bulk of combat operations. To this end, little attention was given to preparing and deploying the kinds of forces best suited to counter-insurgency and mountain warfare, something that proved a crucial liability when the reality failed to match the plan.

For both political and military reasons, though, the elimination of Amin and seizure of the main government buildings in Kabul were essential for the mission. Replacing Amin with Karmal would allow the invasion to be presented as a response to an invitation by the PDPA regime, and meant that DRA forces could be stood down by their own command structures. At the very least, by seizing the DRA's High Command and its central communications nodes, it would prevent any coordinated resistance. Without the special operation which became known as *Shtorm-333* – Storm-333 – then this risked becoming a contested invasion and a three-cornered war between the Soviets, the DRA and the rebels.

Karmal's effective exile to Czechoslovakia had pleased neither him nor Amin. He wanted to be back in Kabul; Amin wanted him dead. Indeed, Amin sent a hit squad to kill him, a plot foiled by the StB, the Czechoslovak equivalent of the KGB. They relocated Karmal and his family first to a sanatorium in a remote mountain village and then an abandoned villa previously used by the Soviet military. Meanwhile, to put Amin's assassins off the trail, the StB conducted a deception operation, getting Karmal to write two postcards mentioning that he was leaving the country, and making sure that the Afghans intercepted them. Karmal was petitioning the Soviets for help toppling Amin and establishing a *Parcham* government, so he was very willing to play the role the KGB had written for him. On 7 December, he and his wife were smuggled back to Afghanistan on an undeclared flight, protected by a team of KGB *Alfa* anti-terrorist commandos under Captain Valentin Shergin, a professional athlete turned bodyguard. They stayed hidden amongst a regiment of Soviet paratroopers based at Bagram air force base in special hides built to resemble regular military shipping containers, until it was time for Karmal to be unveiled as the new Afghan leader.

THE DRA MILITARY

On paper, the DRA had a strong military, but the gap between theoretical and real capability was becoming increasingly wide. It is not that it lacked soldiers willing to fight and units able to demonstrate effectiveness in the field, but rather that they were an increasingly overstretched minority within the armed forces as a whole. The bulk was made up of conscripts serving three-year terms, although draft-dodging was rife and would become even more of a problem from 1980. Morale was low, conditions were poor, and troops largely made do with out-of-date Soviet weaponry.

The army was made up of three army corps, together comprising 14 divisions, of which 11 were infantry and three armoured. However, these units were always chronically under-strength. An infantry division had an establishment strength of just under 8,000, but by 1979 would typically be at close to 2,500. In practice, the main operational units at Amin's disposal were his special forces: the 26th Airborne Battalion and the 37th, 38th and 444th Commando Brigades, although the three 'brigades' were really at no more than regimental strength. Nonetheless, distinguished by camouflage uniforms rather than the army's grey, and with a certain esprit de corps, the commandos proved willing to take the fight to the *mujahideen* in a way most army units would not. As for the 26th Airborne Battalion, despite its name, it never made a combat parachute drop, and would mutiny in 1980, leading to its dissolution.

The air force was likewise small and poorly equipped, and its better-educated officers were mistrusted by Amin as many held *Parchami* sympathies (and had also trained in the Soviet Union). Even before the Soviet invasion, most flight crews were not considered either well-enough trained or well-enough motivated to carry out strikes against the rebels, and the Soviets initially grounded the entire air force until it had carefully screened its officers. Given that the majority of the DRA's fleet of aged MiG-21 fighters, Su-7 and Su-17 fighter-bombers and L-39 trainers were inoperable because of poor maintenance or a lack of certified flight crews, this was no great loss.

There was also an array of security forces, as befitted Amin's paranoia and his desire to have agencies watch and check other agencies. The Ministry of Tribes and Frontiers controlled the Border Troops and a tribal militia that theoretically could field 20,000 men. In practice, these were largely either the retinues of local tribal warlords whose loyalties were deeply suspect or else existed only on paper as part of widespread embezzlement schemes. More serious was the Interior Ministry's paramilitary gendarmerie, the *Sarandoy*, or 'Defenders of the Revolution'. This force of 35,000 men was essentially a *Khalqi* militia. They were better paid than the army, and some of them would prove effective fighters, although many were little more than thugs.

The KGB's initial plan

Originally, the KGB – especially Lieutenant General Ivanov – had planned a rather less extensive operation than that which eventually toppled Amin. It pivoted on the existing presence in Kabul of a Soviet special operations

Just as Storm-333 would depend on special forces, so too would the following war. The KGB *Zenit* commando team was later reconfigured as *Kaskad* for continued operations in Afghanistan, and grew from a single unit to a series of locally based ones. Here, a squad from its Badakhshan Operational-Combat Group under Igor Morozov, is on patrol in the mountains. (VoennayPesnay1/CC-SA 3.0)

On the first anniversary of the *Saur* Revolution, on 28 April 1979, the *Khalq* flag flies over the gate of the Arg, still at the time the presidential palace until Amin moved his residency to the Tajbeg Palace. (S. Sobolev/AFP via Getty Images)

force, the so-called Muslim Battalion. More formally the 154th OSN (Special Purpose Detachment), it ironically owed its genesis to Amin himself. In response to Moscow's concerns that deploying Soviet troops into Afghanistan risked alienating locals and triggering a US response, he suggested in spring 1979 that a unit be raised of soldiers from Soviet Central Asia, mainly Uzbeks, Tajiks and Turkmens, who could be passed off as Afghans. (The only Slavs in the unit ended up being the technical specialists in the gun crews of its self-propelled anti-air systems.)

In autumn 1979, then, the Soviet military began to do just that, under the personal supervision of Army General Pyotr Ivashutin, the head of the GRU military intelligence directorate, which controlled the *Spetsnaz* special forces.[2] They began drawing on officers and men, ideally from the *Spetsnaz* and VDV paratroopers, but in some cases from wherever in the Soviet military they could find the right candidates. By 1 June, they had been selected, and soon they began training together at a base in Chirchik, receiving unit certification on 15 July.

The battalion was commanded by Major Khabibzhan Kholbayev, a well-regarded *Spetsnaz* commander from Tashkent who had risen in the 15th *Spetsnaz* Brigade. It reached a strength of 520 officers and men equipped as a light motor rifle (mechanized) battalion. Given their role, they lacked the anti-tank and mortar platoons of a regular motor rifle battalion, and fielded a mix of BMP tracked infantry

2 See Mark Galeotti, *Spetsnaz: Russia's special forces*, Elite 206 (2015)

fighting vehicles and BTR-60 wheeled armoured personnel carriers (APCs), where usually a battalion would standardize on one or the other. They wore Afghan army uniforms which had had to be made specially from cloth bought in Afghanistan and smuggled to the Soviet Union by GRU agents. Because they had to blend in with regular DRA troops, they were equipped to rather dated standards for *Spetsnaz*, who would normally receive the best. This meant using 7.62mm AK-47 and AKM-47 rifles instead of the 5.45mm AK-74s which by then were becoming the standard in Soviet use, and neither helmets nor body armour. The Muslim Battalion was flown to Kabul's Bagram military airbase on 9–10 December, following a Politburo resolution of 6 December, ostensibly to provide additional security for Amin.

The idea was that the Muslim Battalion, along with operators from a KGB force known as *Zenit*, described below, and the two battalions of paratroopers based at Bagram airbase, would be enough. Amin would be killed by *Zenit* snipers while heading out from the so-called 'Objective *Dub*' ('Oak'), the Arg, his palace in south-central Kabul. Then the Soviet forces would seize the rest of the city in the ensuing chaos, aided by a spontaneous rising against the regime, and install Karmal.

This was ridiculously under-planned and over-optimistic. The consensus amongst those who would have been called on to execute it was that it was the work of people who had little real knowledge of special operations. Major Yakov Semyonov, one of the commanders of the *Zenit* force and a former tactics instructor at KUOS, the KGB's special operations training programme, warned that, for example, it presumed 22 KGB *Spetsnaz* and a single company of the Muslim Battalion, could take on the more than

Paratroopers would provide essential extra firepower to Storm-333, not least thanks to their BMD IFVs. Here, a platoon of VDV are shown in the assault; note their AK-74 rifles and distinctive berets. It was standard practice for them to dismount from their BMD IFVs and attack on foot, while their carriers assumed the role of accompanying fire support vehicles. (Russian Ministry of Defence/CC 4.0)

2,000 defenders of Amin's palace. Another *Zenit* officer later recalled the naïve expectations of Ivanov's plan, which would have been disastrous had it been attempted:

> Supposedly local people were anxiously waiting at these facilities for us to show up; all of them there would surrender to us and come out with hands raised. They wouldn't even shoot. Moreover, all the people were ready to rise up then and there to fight the Amin regime; we needed only to appear at the outskirts of the city and we would be joined by huge masses of people ready to throw out the rotten tyrant and his henchmen. Everything had been looked after and arranged.

The plan was due to be implemented on 13 December. General Magometov was only briefed about the plan the evening before, though, and was horrified. He felt that this operation had no chance of success and would only ruin Soviet–Afghan relations, especially as the political operation to replace Amin seamlessly with Karmal had not been prepared. Next morning, he confronted Ivanov and also called the General Staff in Moscow. After a day of furious behind-the-scenes negotiation, recrimination and retraction, the operation was called off, although a fall-back KGB assassination operation was already in play. In any case, that failed. Amin and his cousin Asadullah Amin, head of the KAM secret police, drank the poisoned cola intended to kill them, but it turned out that the drink's carbonation diluted the agent. Amin was unharmed and Asadullah fell ill with what appeared to be hepatitis, but only the next day. Ironically enough, he was sent for treatment in the USSR. After the eventual coup, he was initially held in the KGB's notorious Lefortovo prison in Moscow, before being deported back to Afghanistan, where the new government wasted no time in having him executed.

Karmal was quietly evacuated back to Tashkent in Soviet Turkestan, and a more extensive and complex plan began to be prepared. First of all, extra troops were brought in. On 14 December, another battalion of the 345th Guards Independent Air Assault Regiment was deployed to Bagram along with a reconnaissance company, to reinforce the battalion of the 111th Guards Air Assault Regiment (105th Guards Airborne Division) which had been based there since July to provide security for the airbase and the Soviet transport aircraft there. This and subsequent measures were sold to Amin as a limited response to his request for Soviet forces on the ground to protect him and his regime. Thus, on 17 December, the Muslim Battalion was redeployed from Bagram to provide additional security for the Dar-ul Aman Palace, the General Staff building, which was in the centre of a cluster of other government buildings including the parliament. This provided a great location inside the security perimeter and also an opportunity to scout out the inner defences.

Enter Kolesnik

More to the point, responsibility for developing the plan to remove Amin was given to a real specialist. This was Colonel Vasily Kolesnik from the

5th Directorate of the GRU (military intelligence). He was a career *Spetsnaz* special forces officer, previously commander of the 15th Special Designation Brigade in Turkestan before transferring to the GRU's central HQ in the so-called 'Aquarium' at Khodinka in north-western Moscow. Given that many of the assets in the field were their special forces, as his deputy, Kolesnik was assigned Colonel Yuri Drozdov of the KGB's First Chief Directorate (PGU), its foreign intelligence arm. Drozdov was head of the PGU's Department S, which ran undercover agents in the field, and Andropov and PGU chief Vladimir Kryuchkov personally sent him to Kabul undercover on 19 December. The other members of Kolesnik's planning team were GRU Lieutenant Colonel Oleg Shvets, his other deputy, and Captain Second Rank Evald Kozlov, a former naval officer who had then transferred to the KGB and been training its special operations assets.

The official portrait of Vasily Kolesnik, the *Spetsnaz* officer and staffer from the GRU's 5th Directorate who was selected by military intelligence chief General Ivashutin to head the Storm-333 operations team. (Author's Collection)

Kolesnik flew to Afghanistan on 16 December, and he quickly locked horns with Magometov and Ivanov, the chief Soviet military adviser to the DRA and the KGB *resident*, respectively. Ivanov was supportive of the notion of intervention, but hoped to have a greater role in it; Magometov was less keen to see an invasion unless it was truly overwhelming in its scale. More generally, though, this was also a product of the very hierarchical nature of the Soviet system: the two generals proved much less deferential to a mere colonel than they had to General Kirpichenko, even though he was essentially making the same points. Instead, Kolesnik had to go over their heads to Ogarkov, and with the Chief of the General Staff's blessing, he arranged for more forces, including paratroopers equipped with heavy weapons, to be added to the operation.

Nonetheless, the main assets were already on the ground, the Muslim Battalion and a team of KGB operators from KUOS (*Kursy usovershenstvovaniya ofitserskogo sostava*), the 'Officer Development Courses' that were actually that agency's specialist training for saboteur and special tactics teams. KUOS training had been running since 1966, first at the KGB Higher School, and then at a specialized facility at Balashikha, outside Moscow. It was a special project of the 8th Section of the PGU's Department S, with a seven-month syllabus covering a range of mayhems, from building and using improvised explosive devices to wilderness survival, as well as parachuting and advanced physical conditioning. The aim was to develop a cadre of serving and reserve KGB officers who could be used for sabotage and assassination missions deep in an enemy's rear, or else to raise and lead partisan units behind an invader's front line. About 60 officers graduated from KUOS each year. In July 1979, though, a small team of KUOS graduates personally selected by KGB Colonel Grigory Boyarinov, the head of the programme, had been sent to Kabul and attached to the Soviet embassy there under the cover of its school. This team was assigned

The mouth of the Salang Tunnel, a crucial connection to the Soviet Union, and one of the reasons why it was so important to act with surprise, as it was also a bottleneck for any invasion along the north-eastern axis. (Michal Vogt/CC-SA 2.0)

the codename *Zenit* ('Zenith'). At that time, it was thought their missions might include anything from diplomatic security to hostage rescue. As planning for Storm-333 began the team was slowly expanded from its initial ten men to fully 150, based in three villas rented by the embassy. *Zenit*'s field commander was Colonel Alexei Polyakov, another of the KUOS instruction faculty.

It was also supplemented by another KGB unit. This, with the callsign *Grom* ('Thunder'), was a 24-strong special operations team under Major Mikhail Romanov drawn from *Alfa*, the KGB's specialized anti-terrorist commando force, which had been established by Yuri Andropov in 1974, following the terrorist massacre at the 1972 Munich Olympics. Rather than the Ninth Directorate, which handled VIP security, it was part of the Seventh Directorate, which was a specialized surveillance service, reflecting the notion that *Alfa* ought to be able to conduct covert operational intelligence-gathering as well as direct attacks.

The 345th Guards Independent Air Assault Regiment under Lieutenant Colonel Nikolai Serdyukov had also been based at Bagram airbase, 90km outside Kabul, since the beginning of December, under the guise of providing security for Soviet airlift assets there. Its 9th Company under Senior Lieutenant Valery Vostrotin, who would emerge as one of the most decorated soldiers of the Afghan War, would be assigned to the assault force, to provide both additional troops and also heavy fire support, notably anti-tank missiles.

With the land routes subject to constant threat of mines and ambushes, the Soviets depended heavily on their airbridges back to the USSR, especially Bagram airbase. The image from later in the war – evident from the new-pattern 'Afghan' battledress the Soviet soldier in the foreground is wearing – also shows the Il-76 transport aircraft that were such a mainstay of the war, along with the An-12 'Black Tulips' that brought the bodies of fallen servicemen home. (E. Kuvakin/CC-SA 3.0)

THE PLAN

However tall the mountain, there's a road to the top of it.

Afghan proverb

In theory, the Soviets were developing plans to protect Amin. In practice, Kolesnik already had a good sense that things were heading in a different direction and prepared accordingly. First of all, he put a much greater emphasis on quickly gathering detailed intelligence of the target, especially as the initial plan had been based on Amin being resident at the Arg but, as will be discussed below, on 16 December, he decided to move to the Tajbeg Palace, instead. A whole variety of opportunities were taken to reconnoitre target locations and test the readiness and posture of the guards. Polyakov's team had also been in-country for months and had compiled extensive files which provided Kolesnik's team an invaluable basis for their planning.

When Amin decided to move his residence to the Tajbeg Palace, this effort went into high gear. Oleg Balashov, one of the *Grom*'s section commanders, played the role of a Soviet diplomatic bodyguard to accompany several delegations to the Tajbeg Palace, for example. Most enterprisingly, on seeing that a nearby hotel's restaurant had an excellent panoramic view of the palace grounds, *Zenit*'s Major Semyonov and his *Grom* counterpart, Major Romanov, along with two *Grom* operators, visited the day before the operation and took detailed pictures. They were subsequently stopped from returning to their barracks by a DRA security patrol and questioned, but they were able to convince them that they had simply been considering it as a venue for a New Year's Eve party.

The real trump card, though, was that while Amin's personal security team was recruited from his relatives and closest supporters, they were provided with technical support by a team from the KGB's Ninth Directorate, the unit which provided security for Party officials and key Soviet government buildings. The head of this team, Major Yuri Kutepov, not only provided a detailed floorplan of the palace, he was also able

KEY FIGURES OF STORM-333

Command team

Colonel Vasily Kolesnik, Fifth Directorate, GRU

Colonel Yuri Drozdov, Head of Department S, KGB First Chief Directorate

Captain 2nd Rank Evald Kozlov, Department S, KGB First Chief Directorate

Grom

Major Mikhail Romanov, field commander

Major Viktor Karpukhin, section commander

Captain Oleg Balashov, section commander

Zenit

Colonel Grigory Boyarinov, head of KUOS

Colonel Alexei Polyakov, field commander

Major Yakov Semyonov, section commander

Muslim Battalion

Major Khabibzhan Kholbayev, commander

Captain Makhmud Sakhatov, deputy commander

Captain Abdulkasym Ashurov, chief of staff

Senior Lieutenant Khamid Abdullayev, political officer

9th Company, 345th Guards Independent Air Assault Regiment

Senior Lieutenant Valery Vostrotin, commander

to provide invaluable details about guard shifts, alarms, and even the personal habits of the members of Amin's security detail. He even found a pretext to get Drozdov into the building to make his own sketches and observations.

From Oak to hill

After all, in mid-December, Amin, perhaps sensing something in the air, had chosen to move his residence from the Arg to the Tajbeg Palace. On the face of it, this made the mission of Storm-333 all the more difficult, as the palace's defences were formidable. Some 16km (10 miles) from the centre of Kabul, the palace was built in the 1920s as part of King Amanullah Khan's drive to modernize Afghanistan, along European lines. It sat upon a natural knoll, which had been shaped into terraces, so that access was either up steep and exposed wide steps at either end, or along a curving roadway. Beyond some trees – which were largely bare in winter anyway – the area within the outer paths was essentially open, and thus easy to survey and open to the fire of the emplaced defences. Areas away from the main roads and barracks were also mined.

Mohammed Daoud Khan (right), meeting General Mohammed Asif Safi. Daoud's seizure of power inadvertently brought Soviet intervention closer by pushing the PDPA towards launching a coup of its own. Had Amin stayed in the palace he ultimately inherited from Daoud, maybe he would not have shared his fate. (Safi1919/CC 3.0)

The palace was guarded by a mix of Amin's personal security team, mechanized security forces, and *Sarandoy*, the 'Defenders of the Revolution' paramilitary security police. The palace building was guarded inside and out by Amin's 40-strong plain-clothes protection team and a company of the Presidential Security Detachment, whose barracks were close by. They could be distinguished from regular DRA troops by their white cap facings, belts and cuff piping. Along with the *Sarandoy*, they also manned a series of fortified checkpoints on the main access routes to the palace. Three T-54 tanks were also dug in at the back of the palace.

A second security perimeter was originally to have been provided by a battalion of the DRA army's Security Brigade, but in a stroke of good fortune for them, the Soviets were able to persuade Amin that it made more sense to use the Muslim Battalion, instead. Amin's paranoia for once made Moscow's job easier. Worried by the threat of coups from his own soldiers, Amin was happy to bring the Soviet forces close to the palace, so much so that they had to move into unfinished barracks 700m (766 yards) from the palace that didn't even have glass in their windows, a particular challenge given that on a winter night, the temperature in Kabul regularly drops to -20°C (-4°F). The soldiers ended up tacking sheets cut from tents over the openings, and even had to fly wood in from the Soviet Union for their stoves, so inefficient was the local logistical support structure.

This image gives a good sense of how the Tajbeg Palace looked before Storm-333. Ironically, having badly damaged it during the operation, the Soviets then rebuilt the palace, so that it could become the 40th Army's headquarters. It was only to be broken, looted and bombarded again during the civil war that rocked Afghanistan in the 1990s. (Mikhail Evstafiev/CC-SA 3.0)

Nonetheless, this was done on 21 December, ensuring that when Storm-333 was launched, there would already be two companies of Soviet *Spetsnaz* inside the perimeter (generally they rotated one company at a time on guard duty, but the operation was timed during shift change).

This also meant that Kolesnik and his team could meet the heads of the DRA Security Brigade and assess the situation on the ground. Colonel Kolesnik went under the cover identity of 'Major Kolesov', the battalion's deputy commander for combat training, Lieutenant Colonel Shvets became 'Major Shvetsov', a political officer, and the KGB's Colonel Drozdov was introduced as 'Captain Lebedev', the battalion technical lead, and faced some ribbing from the Afghans for the fact that he was so old still to be a captain.

Beyond the Muslim Battalion's perimeter were the remaining elements of the Security Brigade: three infantry battalions and an armoured battalion equipped with 30 T-62 tanks. The latter was under-strength by Soviet standards, with just three companies instead of the usual four, but potentially formidable, nonetheless. Against the risk of threats from the air, a regiment with 12 100mm KS-19 anti-aircraft guns were emplaced on a knoll near the palace, as well as 16 ZPU-2 mounts with twin 14.5mm KPV autocannon.

The overall commander was Major Sabri Jandad, commander of the Security Brigade. The Soviets knew him well, as he had trained in the USSR, graduating from the Odessa Anti-Aircraft Artillery School. He spoke good Russian and was also able to hold his own in the usual vodka-fuelled drinking sessions familiar to Soviet officers. He was

The 100mm KS-19 anti-aircraft gun was dated by 1979 but still potentially lethal if the battery defending the Tajbeg Palace had been brought to bear on the attacks. (Museum of Russian Military History/CC-SA 4.0)

considered a serious and dedicated officer, as well as one of Amin's most trusted men: it was a unit under his command, for example, that had murdered Taraki. According to some sources, there was even some consideration by the KGB as to whether it was wise to try and suborn or even eliminate him beforehand, but ultimately it was felt that there was too great a risk that this would tip off the Afghans ahead of time.

In total, then, the palace was defended by some 2,500 soldiers and security personnel, with the potential for reinforcements from a construction battalion on the outskirts of the palace, two tank brigades, the 4th and 15th, stationed nearby, as well as Kabul's army garrison and *Sarandoy* command. Against this, the Soviets planned to field not even a quarter as many soldiers. To have any chance of success, they would need surprise – and cunning.

The KGB's headquarters in Moscow, the infamous Lubyanka. From here, Yuri Andropov had dispatched both the *Grom* and *Zenit* teams who would play such a crucial role in Storm-333. Likewise, here many of the lessons of the operation, and especially the value of surprise and misdirection, were most keenly assessed. (Author's Collection)

The assault force

On 23 December, Magometov formally asked Kolesnik to draw up a plan instead to seize the Tajbeg Palace and remove Amin. He had been expecting it, but nonetheless spent the night preparing his formal proposals, that were approved the next day. Magometov initially offered him just a single company of the Muslim Battalion but Kolesnik demanded – and got – the full unit. This means that, in total, the Soviet forces assigned to neutralize the security forces, seize the palace and remove Amin numbered around 661 men: 24 operators from *Grom*, 30 from *Zenit*, 520 *Spetsnaz* in the Muslim Battalion and 87 paratroopers from the 345th Regiment. That said, some elements were not involved in the actual fighting, so the actual field force was closer to 560. They were divided into 12 ad hoc teams.

THE ATTACK

BG1

BG6

BG10

BG2

3rd Security Bn
Construction Bn

TAJBEG PALACE

2nd Security Bn

EVENTS

1. Attempted poisoning of Amin
2. BG1 engages 3rd Security Battalion
3. Emplaced tanks neutralised
4. BG2 and BG3 set out for Palace
5. BG2 reaches and assaults Palace
6. Boyarinov killed; BG3 joins assault
7. BG9, BG5 and BG4 launch attacks on southern security units
8. BG6 and BG10 launch attacks on northern security units
9. 3rd Security Battalion suppressed
10. Palace air defences suppressed
11. Amin killed
12. Suppression fire from ZSU-23-4 guns
13. Presidential Security Detachment barracks fall

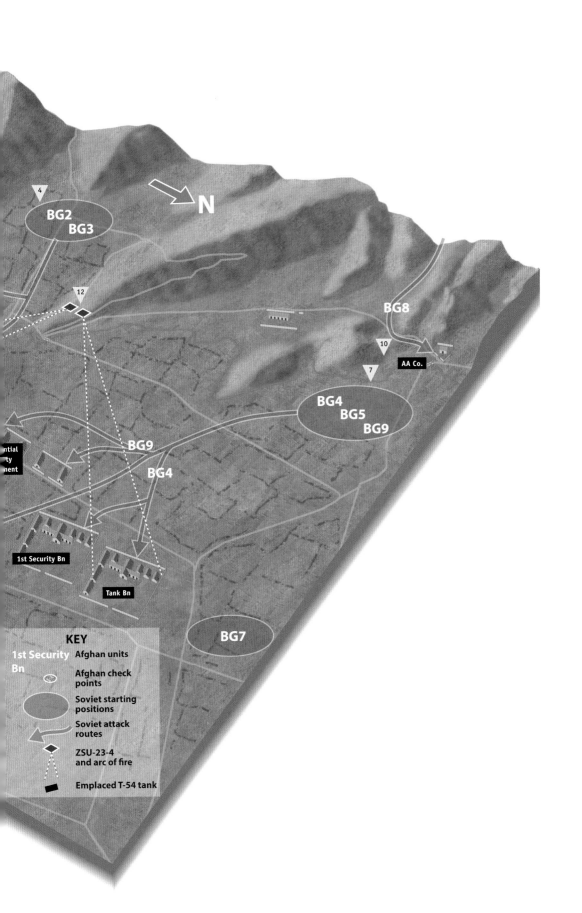

N

BG2
BG3

4

12

BG8

10

7

AA Co.

BG4
BG5
BG9

BG9

BG4

1st Security Bn

Tank Bn

BG7

KEY

1st Security Bn	Afghan units
	Afghan check points
	Soviet starting positions
	Soviet attack routes
	ZSU-23-4 and arc of fire
	Emplaced T-54 tank

The BTR-60PB was cheap and versatile, but it was only lightly armoured and disembarking through its roof hatches could be tricky, especially under fire. Given the risk of mines, when they could, Soviet soldiers in Afghanistan would ride on top. (Russian Ministry of Defence/CC 4.0)

Each such *Boyevaya Gruppa* (BG) – Combat Group – had its own special mission and its size and equipment was tailored for this purpose.

BG1 under Captain Makhmud Sakhatov, deputy commander of the Muslim Battalion, was tasked with moving in first to neutralize the emplaced tanks blocking and covering the access roads. It therefore was made up of eight two-man anti-tank teams, each armed with an RPG-7 rocket-propelled grenade launcher, as well as eight other soldiers to provide fire support: four riflemen from the battalion's 3rd Company, as well as four snipers; two operators from *Zenit* and two from *Grom*. The KGB operators in the assault force were wearing Afghan uniforms, but had altered them with larger pockets for grenades and extra magazines and similar personal touches. More importantly, most were equipped with helmets and 6B1 armoured vests, a bulky item first issued in 1957, but the best available to Soviet special forces at the time. Captain Ashur Jamolov, the battalion's intelligence officer, was also attached to this unit.

BG2 was the main assault force, and as such was commanded by Colonel Boyarinov himself, who had arrived the day before to take personal charge of 'his boys' from KUOS. He was assisted by Senior Lieutenant Sharipov of the Muslim Battalion's 3rd Company and also Captain Second Rank Evald Kozlov. Mounted in the 3rd Company's six BMP infantry fighting vehicles, BG2's 30 fighters were meant to take out the guard posts on the main access route and stage a frontal assault on the palace. While Muslim Battalion troops operated the BMPs, most of the group was from *Grom*, although they were also accompanied by a KGB Department S officer, Andrei Yakushev, and an Afghan collaborator, former security chief Asadullah Sarwari, as translators in case they needed to bluff their way past security posts. The BMP was the first Soviet tracked infantry fighting vehicle, a lightly armoured and infamously temperamental design armed with a turret-mounted 73mm 2A28 low-pressure gun and a launcher for the 9M14 *Malyutka* (AT-3A Sagger) anti-tank wire-guided missile, as well as a 7.62mm PKT machine gun.

BG3 was tasked with a flank attack on the palace, up the stairs on the east of the building and then in through multiple entrances. Commanded by *Zenit*'s Major Yakov Semyonov, it comprised 34 men mounted in four BTR-60PB APCs. Most were from *Zenit*, but there were also vehicle crewmen from the Muslim Battalion and Said Mohammad Gulyabzoy, an Afghan *Khalqi* and former communications minister, who had nonetheless fallen out with Amin after Taraki's death. The BTR-60PB, an eight-wheel APC, was a fast and agile design, although thinly armoured and only armed with a 14.5mm KPVT heavy machine gun and a 7.62mm PKT machine gun. Nonetheless, unlike the BMP, which could only carry eight soldiers along with its three crew, the BTR-60 could carry 14. Like BG2, they carried scaling ladders in case they had the opportunity to try and gain entry directly to the upper floor of the palace, although in the event they were never used.

The LuAZ-967M was a workhorse for the VDV, a light four-wheel drive utility vehicle that was amphibious, rugged, and light enough to be easily lifted by helicopter or dropped by parachute. It was used for a wide variety of roles, from transporting support weapons and munitions to evacuating casualties. (Alf van Beem/ CC 1.0)

Park Patriot is a massive exercise in Russian military soft power, with a side order of historical revisionism, a virtual theme park outside Moscow next to the Kubinka training ground. It includes an exhibit to the Afghan War to which, as here, teenagers in the Young Army patriotic movement are invited. (Russian Ministry of Defence/ CC 4.0)

BG4 was a large Muslim Battalion unit largely made up of its 1st Company. Its mission was to pen the 1st Security Battalion and the Tank Battalion in their barracks so that they could not prevent the attack on the palace. To this end, it was reinforced with the company's support platoon with three PKM machine-gun teams and three RPG-7s. Likewise BG5, two platoons of paratroopers from the 9th Company of the 345th regiment under Senior Lieutenant Valery Vostrotin, were charged with blocking and neutralizing the 2nd Security Battalion. Meanwhile BG6, two platoons of the Muslim Battalion's 2nd Company, would do the same for the 3rd Security Battalion.

BG7 was a fire-support unit made up of the 345th regiment's anti-tank platoon. With six 9K111 *Fagot* (NATO reporting name AT-4 Spigot) missile launchers, they would occupy a position from which they could engage the 1st, 2nd or Tank Battalions if need be, or else the Presidential Security Detachment's barracks. The *Fagot* ('Bassoon') was a second-generation wire-guided system with a maximum range of 2,500m, able to defeat the armour of any DRA vehicles in service, including the T-62 tanks of the palace security detail.

BG8, under Lieutenant Colonel Shvets, would engage and suppress the anti-aircraft regiment to ensure it could not deploy its potentially devastating firepower against the attackers. It comprised an infantry platoon of the Muslim Battalion's 3rd Company and a platoon of six AGS-17 automatic grenade launchers.

BG9, the 3rd Platoon of the 345th Regiment's 9th Company, was tasked with engaging the Presidential Security Detachment's barracks and ensuring reinforcements could not reach the palace. It was reinforced with the company's grenade launcher squad with two AGS-17s mounted in a LuAZ-967M light utility vehicle. Similarly, BG10, the 1st Platoon of the Muslim Battalion's 2nd Company, was responsible for suppressing the Afghan army Construction Battalion that was based alongside the 3rd Security Battalion. While essentially a support unit, often busy simply keeping the palace grounds tidy, it did have an armoury and could in theory have provided reinforcements for the palace or obstacles to the attackers' withdrawal, were it allowed to react to the assault.

BG11 was another support unit, fielding four ZSU-23-4 tracked self-propelled anti-air systems, whose quad 23mm cannon would be used to provide direct fires to suppress defenders, even those under cover. Called the 'Shilka' by the Soviets, the ZSU-23-4 was only lightly armoured, but the accuracy and high rate of fire of its water-cooled 23mm 2A7 guns, with a cyclic rate of 850–1,000 rounds per minute – earning it the nickname of the 'sewing machine' – meant that it could be devastating to infantry, lightly armoured targets and even buildings. The first of these systems would support BG2 and BG3 in their assault on the palace, while the rest were put in overwatch to help suppress the main security units: the second was assigned to BG4 and BG7, the third to BG5 and the fourth to BG6.

BG12 likewise was a Muslim Battalion heavy weapons company divided between teams fielding AGS-17 *Plamya* ('Flame') automatic grenade launchers, attached to individual combat groups. Fully eight AGS-17 teams were deployed in support of the main assault on the palace by BG2 and BG3. Another eight were divided in pairs to BG4 and BG7, BG5, BG6 and BG9. The AGS-17 was a substantial weapon, weighing in at 31kg (68lb), but it could fire its 30mm VOG-17M high-explosive fragmentation rounds out to 1,700m (1,859 yards), and its capacity to be elevated to loft its rounds in indirect fire over obstacles allowed them to dominate the whole area around the palace.

Finally, there were several command units and a recovery and evacuation platoon. While Boyarinov had chosen to lead from the front, a decision that would cost him his life, overall command of the operation was carried out by Colonels Kolesnik and Drozdov, along with the Muslim Battalion's Major Kholbayev and a KGB liaison officer, Senior Lieutenant

ORBAT OF STORM-333

BG	Commander	Soldiers	Vehicles
1	Capt. SAKHATOV	17 (Sakhatov, 8 two-man RPG-7 Teams, 4 Muslim Bn, 2 *Grom*, 2 *Zenit*)	5 GAZ-66
2	Col. BOYARINOV	32 (Boyarinov, Kozlov, 22 *Grom*, 6 Muslim Bn, 1 KGB, 1 Afghan)	6 BMP-1
3	Maj. SEMYONOV	34 (27 *Zenit*, 6 Muslim Bn, 1 Afghan)	4 BTR-60PB
4	Capt. KUDRATOV	110 (Kudratov, 1 Muslim Bn company)	12 BTR-60PB
5	Sr. Lt. VOSTROTIN	59 (Vostrotin, command squad, 2 paratrooper platoons with 23 men each)	6 BMD-1, 1 BMD-1K, 1 BTR-D
6	Sr. Lt. AMANGELDYEV	58 (2 Muslim Bn platoons with 28 men each)	6 BTR-60PB
7	Sr. Lt. SEVOSTYANOV	19 (Sevostyanov, 6 three-man ATGM teams)	4 GAZ-66A
8	Lt. Col. SHVETS	47 (Shvets, 1 Muslim Bn platoon with 28 men, 6 three-man AGS-17 teams)	4 BMP-1, 3 UAZ-469
9	N/a	26 (paratrooper platoon, grenade launcher squad)	3 BMD-1, 1 LuAZ-967M
10	Lt. NURITDINOV	57 (2 Muslim Bn platoons)	6 BTR-60PB
11	Sr. Lt. PRAUTA	16 (4 four-man vehicle crews)	4 ZSU-23-4
12	Sr. Lt. MIRYUSUPOV	25 (Miryusupov, 8 three-man AGS-17 crews)	4 BTR-60PB
HQ/Support	Col. KOLESNIK	59 (nine-man command team, 2 Muslim Bn sections, medical, engineer and logistics sections)	1 BMP-1K, 1 BMP-1KSh, 2 BMP-1, 1 Zil-131 MTO-AT, 4 Ural-375D

NB: Accounts vary, and this must be considered a speculative ORBAT.

Colonel General Sergei Akhromeyev was one of the first senior Soviet officers to have a sense that Afghanistan and the PDPA were going to be a problem. He would succeed Marshal Ogarkov as Chief of the General Staff in 1984, a position he held until 1988, and thus he was the architect of the careful extrication of Soviet forces from the war. (Russian Ministry of Defence/CC 4.0)

Makhamodzhon Baykhambayev, from a BMP-1K battalion command variant of the regular BMP, fitted with R-123M and R-130 radios. Another command team with the Muslim Battalion's chief of staff, Captain Abdulkasym Ashurov, was mounted in a BMP-1KSh variant, which traded its heavy armament for a communication and sensor suite. Two other BMPs, each with a section of Muslim Battalion riflemen, provided security. A Zil-131 MTO-AT recovery truck and four Ural-375D trucks, as well as a medical team rounded out the force. The 34 men of the Muslim Battalion's Supply and Signal Platoons kept out of the fight, as did the 9th Company's Mortar Platoon.

Parallel to the planning for Storm-333 were the preparations for the main invasion, Operation Baikal-79. In order to maintain strategic surprise, the invasion would largely be carried out by forces from TurkVO or the neighbouring Central Asian Military District. This meant calling up more than 50,000 reservists to bring local units up to full strength. On 12 December, the 108th Motor Rifle Division was brought to combat footing. Its 180th Motor Rifle Regiment deployed close to the border under the guise of a military exercise. Meanwhile, on 13 December, the 5th Guards Motor Rifle Division in Kushka likewise began preparing for action. Later, on 24 December, the 201st Motor Rifle Division based in Dushanbe was also mobilized, so that it could reinforce the 108th.

On 13 December, General Akhromeyev established a special Operations Group bringing together General Staff officers and representatives of all the services involved in the operation. By the next day, it had set up its command centre at Termez, on the Soviet–Afghan border, although soon after Akhromeyev fell ill and was replaced by First Deputy Defence Minister Marshal Sergei Sokolov. Its role was essentially a coordinating one as, on 16 December, the 40th Army was formally stood up as the field command structure for what became known as the 'Limited Contingent of Forces in Afghanistan', originally under TurkVO First Deputy Commander Lieutenant General Yuri Tukharinov.

Meanwhile, by 14 December, the 103rd Guards Air Assault Division had completed a redeployment from its base at Vitebsk in Belarus to airfields in the Turkestan Military District, notably Balkhash in Kazakhstan, ready to be airlifted to Kabul. Elements of Military Transport

Aviation were prepared for this purpose and fuel depots opened to ensure they could fly round the clock.

On 22 December, newly appointed Soviet Ambassador Fikryat Tabeyev had told Amin that the Politburo had approved his request for Soviet troops and that the first would deploy on 25 December. Amin was overjoyed and instructed his military to give the arriving troops every assistance. Mindful of the need for strategic surprise, in a classic example of Soviet *maskirovka* – strategic deception – those moves which could not be explained as preparations to 'support' the Amin regime were presented as a military exercise in TurkVO. Furthermore, the operational orders were delivered by hand to avoid the risk of their being intercepted by Western electronic eavesdropping. Communications by radio or telephone were typically kept brief and avoided any explicit mention of Afghanistan.

On 25 December, just as the first Soviet forces were preparing to enter Afghanistan, Kolesnikov and Magometov had a final secure telephone briefing with Akhromeyev in Moscow. After hearing a detailed summary of Kolesnikov's plan and questioning him about the smallest details, the punctilious Akhromeyev approved Storm-333. As they left, Magometov – who, like Ivanov, refused to sign off on the plan – turned to Kolesnikov and said to him, 'Well, colonel, this will now make you or break you.'

One constraint of Storm-333 was the lack of anything but battlefield fire support. Once the invasion started, the high command made sure it had ample amounts of long-range firepower. Here, a Soviet self-propelled artillery battery deployed to Afghanistan prepares its fire orders. In the background are four 2S1 Gvozdika 122mm guns. (Russian Ministry of Defence/ CC 4.0)

THE RAID

He didn't have time even to scratch his head.

Afghan proverb

Storm-333 was a complex operation that spanned more than just the assault on the Tajbeg Palace. In order to neutralize not just the palace defenders but the DRA's military overall – the aim, after all, was to do as little damage as possible to the security forces that would still have to fight the *mujahideen* – a whole series of diversionary and sabotage operations were launched in concert. In the single evening of 27 December 1979, the central command structure of the country was paralysed and its defenders in the capital penned, captured or killed.

Preparing chaos

Soviet advisers were attached to every substantial DRA unit. Although they were also often watched by the KAM secret police, their presence offered a wide range of opportunities for mischief and misdirection. For example, the advisers attached to the 4th and 15th Armoured Brigades took the opportunity to remove the batteries of many of their tanks in the guise of a maintenance and winterizing programme, so they could not be started. The tank regiment of the 8th Infantry Division was instructed to drain its vehicles of fuel as they were to receive newer models. An inventory of supposedly faulty stocks for the 7th and 8th Divisions ensured that many units had no ammunition to hand, and the Soviet advisers controlled the arsenals.

This image of an abandoned DRA T-55 tank outside Bagram airbase after the Soviet withdrawal illustrates the high mountains around Kabul which would be a constant risk to aviation – as was discovered during the initial airlift. (USAF/Public Domain)

The Afghan armed forces were largely equipped with Soviet hand-me-downs, although the 15th Tank Brigade was equipped with T-62s. This was the most modern tank fielded by the DRA, whose stocks also included T-55s and even World War II-vintage T-34s. (Davric/Public Domain)

Other advisers, such as those attached to 26th Airborne Brigade, made a point of organizing a dinner for the officers of their units, at which plentiful alcohol and rich food would hopefully distract them before the alarm could be raised, leaving them sluggish and befuddled thereafter. On the other hand, some advisers – notably those under especially tight KAM surveillance or else who did not have an especially good rapport with their Afghan counterparts – were told to make their excuses and make sure they were away from their units before night fell.

Indeed, Kolesnik even tried to lure away the commanders of the palace's guardians by inviting them to a banquet that evening. Major Jandad, though, was too professional, and said that his officers could only come in the evening after their shifts were over. He did allow the Soviet military advisers attached to the guard units to leave early, though, and this may well have saved them from any reprisals or being used as hostages that night. Nonetheless, this may have aroused suspicions, because later that afternoon, Muslim Battalion picquets reported that Jandad was personally inspecting their positions. Kolesnik had originally been thinking of launching the operation at 9:30pm, but as a result of this intelligence, the decision was made to bring it forward. In fairness, though, it could just as easily have been that Jandad was spooked by the attempted poisoning of Amin, discussed below.

Ismail Murtuza Ogly Aliyev, the head of the KGB department in Afghanistan responsible for supporting the activities of Soviet 'illegals' – undercover agents – was especially heavily involved in a series of other activities to maximize Storm-333's chances. Paralysing Afghan communications was a particular priority, especially to prevent reinforcements being called to the palace, and this was a target of 'Operation Well'. For days before, a team of KGB officers under communications specialist Major Boris Pleshkunov had been studying the city's telephone lines (this had been set up by West Germans, and so the Soviets did not already have details) to identify where all the key cables emerged from the main communications centre. They were buried some five metres (16ft) underground, but the Soviets discovered that there was an access point, albeit under a heavy concrete slab. A team from *Zenit*, working with technical specialists from the embassy, drew up a plan, which even involved secretly forging metal tongs of the appropriate length and diameter to be able to lift the slab.

At 7:10pm, shortly before the start of Storm-333, a three-car team of *Zenit* operators and KGB specialists drove to the communications centre. There was a police guard post nearby, so while the Afghans were distracted by two of the agents, the others manhandled open the hatch and lowered a specially made explosive charge into the well below. Along with 40kg (88lb) of high explosive, they threw down a tear-gas grenade – even if the Afghans had realized what was going on and tried to defuse the device, the grenade would have prevented them for the next, crucial few minutes. The Soviets left the scene and, at 7:20pm, the bomb exploded, leaving the entire city without telephone connections.

This was just as well, as Lieutenant Colonel Ahmad Jan, commander of the 15th Tank Brigade, had just been ordered to prepare a battalion to be deployed into Kabul as extra security. The battalion was being readied and Jan was awaiting final confirmation and also specific orders as to where to send them. He waited half an hour before wondering where his orders were, only then discovering that the phone lines were down. Then it took half an hour before the brigade's signals platoon confirmed that this was a general fault – by which time Storm-333 was already under way and it was too late.

A poisonous prelude

The KGB had still not given up on the thought of taking out Amin by poison. Earlier that day, an assassin from Directorate S called Mikhail Talubov had managed to introduce an agent into a vegetable soup. Amin was in good spirits and had organized a lunch for Politburo members of *Khalq* to welcome back from Moscow Ghulam Dastagir Panjsheri, the Chairman of the Party Control Commission, whom he credited with finally persuading the Soviets to commit military forces. Panjsheri had also reassured him that the Soviets had accepted his version of Taraki's death, and were willing to let bygones be bygones. Amin had also just heard that the first Soviet formations had crossed the border, and was claiming that this would turn the tide against the rebels. 'Everything is going fine,' he said.

Famous (near) last words. Amin – and most of his guests – duly enjoyed the poisoned soup. The expectation had been that the toxic agent would take several hours to have an effect, but either this time the concentration was too great or else the soup was too tasty and they ate more than expected. Most

В ЭТОМ ДОМЕ ЖИЛ
ГЕНЕРАЛ-ПОЛКОВНИК

ТУХАРИНОВ
ЮРИЙ
ВЛАДИМИРОВИЧ

AFGAN

1-ый КОМАНДУЮЩИЙ 40й АРМИЕЙ
ОСУЩЕСТВИВШИЙ ВВОД СОВЕТСКИХ
ВОЙСК В АФГАНИСТАН

of the diners very soon began to feel sleepy and experienced convulsions. Amin soon fell into a coma. His wife, Patmanah, alerted his security team, who in turn called the Central Military Hospital and, ironically enough, the clinic at the Soviet embassy. The unfortunate kitchen staff were detained, on general principles. Two Soviet medics arrived: army doctor Colonel Viktor Kuznechenkov and surgeon Anatoly Alekseyev. Given the extreme security of Storm-333, they had no idea that this was a KGB poisoning, let alone that it was a prelude to an assault, and they immediately had Amin's stomach pumped and put him on an intravenous drip. This saved his life – for a while, at least – and by the early evening he was conscious and mobile, albeit still weak. Dr Kuznechenkov stayed on to treat Amin and was tragically killed in the crossfire during the subsequent assault; he was posthumously awarded the Order of the Red Banner.

The poison had not worked as intended, but unlike the earlier operation, Storm-333 was not dependent on such measures. Indeed, even most of its command team had had no idea that a separate Department S operation was under way. It was simply an additional failsafe, and also intended to sow some confusion in the Afghan ranks. In practice, it actually made the operation tougher, arousing Major Jandad's suspicions and forcing the Soviets to strike earlier, bringing *Vremya Ch* – 'Zero Hour' – forward to around 6:30pm.

A memorial plaque to Colonel General Yuri Tukharinov, first commander of the 40th Army, at the Cosmonautics Museum in Kirov. (Geog pic/CC-SA 3.0)

With its quad radar-guided 23mm cannon, the ZSU-23-4 'Shilka' could be a lethal short-range anti-air defence system, but in Afghanistan it would primarily be used as a devastating self-propelled direct-fire support vehicle, able to rake rooftops and hillsides with equal facility. (Sgt. Ryan Ward, USMC/Public Domain)

The Muslim Battalion moves out

Kolesnik had realized that as soon as the Muslim Battalion units deployed around the palace began to move out of their usual positions, this would be noticeable. So, for a few nights before the operation, they had begun establishing a pattern of unpredictable and often noisy activity. They would let off shots, move to new positions, warm up the engines of their personnel carriers, even launch flares at night. The first time they did this, the DRA Security Brigade went on alert, and the searchlights of the anti-air regiment were trained on the Soviets' positions. However, it was explained that this was simply routine combat training, making sure they accustomed themselves to their new duties and the local terrain. After a few such scares, the Afghans became accustomed to what they wrote off as the unusual zeal of the *Spetsnaz*, and beyond asking them to keep their activities a little quieter so as not to disturb Amin's sleep, they let them be.

What that meant was that on the 27th, the start of the operation was not recognized for what it was. BG1 and the palace assault team, BG2 and BG3, were made up of forces already in place on the guard perimeter. Like the rest of the attack force, they wrapped white cloths ripped from bedsheets around their left arms as a recognition signal given that everyone was wearing DRA uniforms. They also had a simple password, the challenge 'Yasha' and the response 'Misha'. As the *Zenit* operators of BG3 next to them ritually urinated on the wheels of their BTR personnel carriers for luck – an old tradition – BG1 got into their GAZ-66 jeeps. Under Captain Sakhatov, they were tasked with the first mission: neutralizing the T-54 tanks dug in to command the palace mount. They set out around 6:20pm.

Their route took them towards the barracks of the 3rd Security Battalion, and as they approached it, they saw that soldiers were being turned out and issued with weapons, part of the enhanced alert procedures Security Brigade commander Major Jandad had ordered after Amin's collapse. Sakhatov felt they could not simply ignore this, even though the tanks were their main priority. Taking advantage of the fact that no one yet knew that an assault was under way, he took a team with him up to the battalion commander and simply seized him and threw him into the back of their car. Then the rest of the group opened fire on the Afghan troops with their assault rifles, throwing them into chaos.

At the same time, the four snipers had taken down the guards around the tanks with AKM-47 rifles fitted with PBS-1 silencers. However, once Sakhatov's men had started shooting, the alarm was raised and the chances of being able to capture the tanks was lost. It was 7:15pm. Kolesnik, back with his HQ team, decided that the time for stealth was over and ordered the tanks destroyed by direct fire from ZSU-23-4 Shilkas and AGS-17 grenade launchers. Two red flares were fired to signal the start of the wider assault. BG1 continued to engage the security troops, a rather uneven contest once the DRA troops had regrouped in which one *Grom* operator, Dmitry Volkov, was killed. However, they did manage to keep them bottled up long enough for BG6 to join the fray.

The frontal assault

Even before Sakhatov had reached the 3rd Battalion's barracks, BG2 and BG3 had set out towards the palace itself. Kozlov had joined BG2 at the last minute, because Boyarinov – who had only arrived the day before and not yet acclimatized to the situation – looked visibly worried. With Drozdov's permission, Kozlov (who was armed only with a Stechkin pistol), added himself to the team so that he could help Boyarinov coordinate the operation, as he knew the other elements of the assault team better.

Boyarinov's men had the unenviable task of making their way up the access road that looped round the knoll. *Grom* section commander Oleg Balashov, who had been responsible for assigning soldiers to the BMP IFVs (Infantry Fighting Vehicles) that BG2 was mounted in, rightly predicted that the defenders would initially target the first and last of their six-vehicle convoy in the hope of immobilizing them. Given the relatively light armour and fragile track assemblies of the BMPs, he knew they were unlikely to be able to weather the storm of fire they would receive. Thus, he took the first BMP himself. They

The BMP-1 IFV was in many ways a typically Soviet design, prioritizing speed and firepower over protection and comfort. Nonetheless, in Storm-333 they largely managed the difficult task of getting the KGB commandos up to the palace. (Russian Ministry of Defence/CC 4.0)

The defence of the Tajbeg Palace showed the DRA forces at once at their best and their worst. They could be brave and aggressive, as in this attack, but their morale also often proved brittle. (Russian Ministry of Defence/CC 4.0)

headed out at around 7:30pm, in an operation whose main phase would ultimately last only some 45 minutes, although mopping up took until 11pm.

Surprise allowed them to blow past the first checkpoint along the road without any trouble, running over a soldier trying to close the barrier and raking the blockhouse with fire as they passed. By the second, though, the alarm had been raised and they faced active opposition, gunfire hammering on the IFVs' armour. They returned fire through the gunports in the side of the vehicles – accuracy was almost impossible, but they hoped to rattle the defenders and force them to take cover – and the vehicles filled with choking fumes from their Kalashnikovs. Nearing the third, as they rounded the hill, a rocket-propelled grenade disabled Balashov's BMP and he and his squad dismounted and continued on foot. They took heavy fire and all were wounded, but their helmets and body armour helped protect them. Another BMP, commanded by Muslim Battalion political officer Senior Lieutenant Khamid Abdullayev, was hit and damaged. It stalled, but was able to be restarted. Nonetheless, this delayed it and, along with a trailing BTR from BG3 which had followed it, was only later able to join the assault.

As they approached the palace, when they could, the BMPs kept up suppressing fire on the palace with their 73mm low-pressure guns and, arguably more usefully, coaxial 7.62mm machine guns. However, much of the time the angle and the scarp face of the knoll meant they were unable to bear on the palace, so instead a ZSU-23-4 from BG11 kept up covering fire, along with AGS-17s from BG12. Soon, a second Shilka was also turned against the defenders. The heavy walls of the palace provided good protection against both the 23mm rounds of the AA guns and fragmentation from 30mm grenades, but they nonetheless forced defenders back from the windows and turned the flagstoned open space around the palace into a killing zone. This meant that many of the defenders who otherwise could have rained gunfire and grenades down on the attackers as they circled the hill were instead forced to take shelter inside. Some did risk it, though, although *Zenit* operator Valery Kurilov recounted coming across several grenades that had been thrown without anyone thinking to remove the arming pin in the heat of the action.

Nonetheless, a third BMP was hit and caught fire and had to be shunted off the side of the road by the vehicle behind it, as its crew bailed out. By the time BG2 was on the last leg of the path to the palace, fully half the unit was dismounted, many wounded but still in the fray. Indeed, as a BMP swivelled to bring its gun to bear on a window from which defenders were firing a machine gun, it managed to crush the feet of two *Grom* operators, Gennady Zudin and Sergei Kuvylin. Despite this, one continued to limp towards the target while the other settled into a firing position and began providing covering fire.

Within ten minutes of setting out, at around 7:40pm, BG2 had reached the palace walls. Valery Yemyshev, commander of the *Grom* platoon, and KGB translator Andrei Yakushev were the first to burst through the main entrance. They ran into not just a hail of fire from soldiers of the Security Brigade and *Sarandoy* paramilitaries, but also shrapnel from hand grenades being dropped from the upper floor. Yakushev was killed instantly, and Yemyshev badly wounded in the hand. However, this provided the time for one of the BMPs still mobile to pull up to the entrance and for Viktor Karpukhin's *Grom* squad to dismount. At Boyarinov's command, they threw grenades into the lobby and simultaneously breached the building through the main entrance, a window to the side, a side door, and a hole blasted into the wall by an RPG-18 disposable anti-tank rocket. At this point they were joined by the *Grom* team from Abdullayev's BMP and also a team of *Zenit* commandos originally meant to have been part of BG3, as well as the two Muslim Battalion crewmen from their BTR. They had taken serious casualties – eight of the 30 members of BG2 had been killed or seriously injured, and almost all the rest sustained at least light wounds – but they were in.

Storming the palace

As the 2BG under the direct command of Colonel Boyarinov approached the palace, it had to eliminate guard positions while under heavy fire. Here, a *Grom* commando prepares to throw an RGD-5 grenade into a shelter being used by defenders from the Security Brigade while in the foreground Boyarinov calls up the unit's BMP personnel carriers for a last dash to the palace entrance. Note the PS-1 suppressor on the grenadier's AKMS – though obviously the time for subtlety is over – and the NSP-3 nightsight on the SVD sniper rifle carried by the lead soldier. The third carries an AK-47. A ZSU-23-4 self-propelled anti-air gun of 11BG has started to lay down withering suppressive fire on the upper storey of the palace with its quad 23mm autocannon. Given that the Soviets jammed all landline and radio traffic during the attack, the defenders have let off a flare in the hope of summoning aid from loyal DRA forces, but they too had been neutralized ahead of time.

Taking the side route

Meanwhile, the four BTR-60PB personnel carriers carrying BG3 had been racing towards the stairs at the east of the palace, hoping to be able to get the *Zenit* operators they were carrying as close as possible before the defenders realized what was happening. The aim was for them to storm the building from the other side as BG2, at the same time. However, it soon came under fire from heavy machine guns manned by members of the Security Brigade who, after all, were amongst the most elite forces of the DRA and had just been enjoined to heightened vigilance by Major Jandad.

The lead vehicle was promptly hit by gunfire which shredded its tyres and damaged its wheel assemblies. It nonetheless managed to coast into the dead zone directly at the foot of the hill and thus out of the defenders' lines of sight and fire. The second was also hit, and caught fire; the driver panicked and drove the vehicle into a drainage ditch. Senior Lieutenant Boris Suvorov, head of the *Zenit* team assigned to BG3, was mortally wounded when 12.7mm rounds fired at relatively short range penetrated this second BTR's thin armour, but most of the rest of the commandos in the first two vehicles were able to dismount safely. The third BTR safely reached the base of the stairs and kept up heavy suppression fire, but for the next ten, long minutes BG3 was virtually pinned down, until fire from AGS-17 grenade launchers killed one DRA machine-gun crew and forced the rest to take cover inside the palace.

The fourth BTR, which had been trailing the combined BG2 and BG3 convoy when it left the Muslim Battalion positions, ended up actually following the rearmost BMP of the other attack. What was presumably a moment of confusion in the heat of battle probably turned out for the best, as it was able to provide covering fire for Lieutenant Abdullayev's IFV as it was trying to restart its engine, and the entire complement of the BTR joined Boyarinov's assault.

Nevertheless, this meant that between the errant BTR and the casualties it had suffered, BG3 was down to little more than half its initial *Zenit* complement. Once it was no longer suicidal to do so, they stormed up the stairs. Although the heavy machine gun (HMG) emplacements were no longer manned, defenders at the windows of the palace continued to fire at the attackers. Meanwhile, the Soviets

In 1986, in recognition above all for its service in Afghanistan, the 108th Neva Twice Red Banner Motor Rifle Division – one of the initial invasion units – was awarded this pennant 'For Bravery'. (Soviet Ministry of Defence/Public Domain)

COLONEL GRIGORY BOYARINOV

Grigory Ivanovich Boyarinov was an example of a particular kind of officer, who rose through the ranks from being a simple draftee, and yet who never lost his taste for being in the thick of the toughest fighting. He was born on 15 November 1922 in Sukromlya, a village in Russia's western Smolensk region. In 1939, he was drafted into the Red Army where he was quickly identified as having officer potential. He was sent to the Cherkassy Infantry School, which became the 2nd Sverdlovsk Military Infantry School, graduating in July 1941 right in time for the German invasion of the USSR. He commanded a mortar platoon in hard fighting on the Tikhvin Salient, and was hospitalized in November from a head wound. He quickly recovered and returned to the fray as a company commander, suffering a serious wound to his left hand in 1942 but nonetheless continuing to fight, acquiring a reputation as an officer who led from the front.

Because of that reputation, as well as his decision to join the Communist Party in 1942, he was transferred to a Border Troops regiment of the NKVD, the political police. By this time, they were essentially being used as shock troops, and again he was in the thick of some of the hardest fighting on the North-western, Leningrad and Second Baltic Fronts. The NKVD was also responsible for raising, training and directing partisan operations, and in 1943 he was made head of a sniper training programme for partisans. He insisted on joining the partisans on their operations behind Axis lines, and one of his units was reportedly responsible for ambushing and wiping out the commanders of an Italian division. By July 1944, he was chief of staff of an infantry battalion of the 9th NKVD Border Regiment on the Leningrad Front, and he continued to serve in the frontier forces after the war until 1948, when he transferred to the central administration of what had become, thanks to the cannibalistic security politics of the Stalin era, the MGB, the Ministry of State Security. He went on to study at the MGB Military Institute, and after he graduated in 1953, he stayed on as an instructor. He was clearly a high-flier, and went on to take an advanced programme at the military's Frunze Military Academy, the General Staff's staff and command college. After a brief spell at the headquarters of what had now become the KGB, the Committee of State Security, in 1961 he took on a teaching position at its F.E. Dzerzhinsky Higher Red Banner School, where his specialities were precisely in covert military – so-called 'diversionary' – operations.

To this end, when the KUOS 'Officer Improvement Courses' were established in 1969 to build up a cadre of serving and reserve officers with the skills and physical conditioning for behind-the-lines partisan and covert assassination and sabotage missions, he was the obvious candidate to head the programme. He never lost his enthusiasm for fieldwork, though. When the KGB began to contemplate its options in summer 1979, drafting most of his KUOS graduating class to Kabul to form the *Zenit* special operations detachment, he had no hesitation – at age 56 – in volunteering first to join them in scouting out the situation, and when that was disallowed, continuing to press for a role in any potential military operations. He was finally sent to Kabul on 26 December, a final mission from which he would not return.

His death through likely friendly fire outside the Tajbeg Palace was a blow to the KGB, although the subsequent Afghan War would provide ample opportunities for a new generation of such specialists to arise. Colonel Boyarinov was posthumously made a Hero of the Soviet Union – the USSR's highest award, comparable to the Victoria Cross – to add to his existing Order of Lenin and Order of the Red Banner. He is buried in Moscow's Kuzminsky cemetery but his name was taken by the KUOS-Vympel Fund, which raises funds for veterans and their dependants, and in 2017 a memorial plaque was placed in his name in Balashikha, close to where the KUOS programme was once operated.

inside the palace were facing very heavy resistance as they sought to battle their way up from the ground floor. Colonel Boyarinov decided he needed to summon the fighters of BG3 to join them, and stepped out onto the porch above the stairs. He walked into the middle of a withering crossfire, and one bullet hit his armoured vest and ricocheted upwards into his neck, killing him almost instantly. To this day it is uncertain – and possibly irrelevant – whether the 7.62mm round which killed him came from an AK-47 fired by an Afghan defender or an identical rifle used by a Soviet attacker, although the suspicion is that it was the latter.

Whether enraged by Boyarinov's death or simply thanks to the ebb and flow of battle, the first *Zenit* commandos of BG3 were able to make it to the porch shortly thereafter, and enter the palace, where they soon connected with the rest of the assault team as they worked their way to the upper floor where Amin's quarters and offices were to be found.

Bottling up the loyalists south of the palace

Once the assault on the palace had started, other combat groups moved out in their missions to neutralize or at least contain various units of defenders that might otherwise seek to reinforce the Tajbeg: the Presidential Security Detachment and the various battalions of the Security Brigade.

The first of these was undoubtedly the priority, given their proximity to the palace and their personal loyalty to Amin. This was entrusted to BG9, a platoon of paratroopers from the 345th Regiment. Along with the fellow-paras of BG5 and the Muslim Battalion troops of BG4, they entered the palace security zone under the pretence of being the relief for the changing of the palace guard. Given that the paratroopers were mounted not only in the ubiquitous GAZ-66 and UAZ-469 utility jeeps but also their distinctive BMD-1 airborne IFVs, by no means standard kit for DRA forces, it is surprising that they were able to enter the area without challenge or greater scrutiny. One assumption heard among circles of *afgantsy* – veterans of the war – is that either the KGB or GRU had suborned the officers in charge of the main entrance, who were instructed to turn a blind eye or two.

Once through the outer perimeter checks, BG9, mounted in three BMDs and a LuAZ-967M utility carrier, drove towards the barracks as quickly as they could without arousing too much suspicion. Once the firing had begun

The front view of a BMD-1 demonstrates its low and angular profile, reflecting the design priorities of mobility and portability. (Author's Collection)

on the other side of the palace, though, they instead rushed the last couple of minutes of their journey at full speed and were able to take up positions around the barracks, emplacing two RPK machine guns to cover the main doors, and a third to cover the rear, in case people tried to escape through the windows. More significant was the firepower provided by their BMDs which, as well as the same low-pressure 73mm gun as the BMP, mounted three 7.62mm PKT machine guns, one in the turret and two in the bows. Their orders were to prevent any break-out towards the palace, and over the next hour most of the Afghans would flee in the darkness, in ones and twos. So long as they were headed away from the palace and were neither in any numbers or seemed to be trying to move heavy weapons, the paratroopers largely let them go.

The ZPU-2 mount with its twin 14.5mm KPV heavy machine guns was a dated design, even by 1979 – it had first been introduced in 1949 – but it remains in use to this day because it is as effective as a direct-fire ground support weapon as in its original low-level anti-air role. (Derzsi Elekes Andor/ CC-SA 3.0)

When BG9 peeled off at the first sound of the gunfire, Senior Lieutenant Vostrotin's two platoons, in six BMDs, continued on towards the 2nd Security Battalion barracks. The barracks were arranged around a small parade ground, and BG5 bypassed the small headquarters building and deployed in front of the main buildings. Dismounting from the BMDs, they raked the barracks with automatic fire, as well as rockets from both RPG-7s and disposable RPG-18s.

Was occupied Afghanistan an ally or a conquered territory? Often the answer was that it was a bit of both, and navigating this complex situation was the job of Soviet ambassador Fikrayt Tabeyev (centre), here pictured with General Viktor Yermakov (on his right), who became the commander of the 40th Army in 1982. (Russian Ministry of Defence/ CC 4.0)

The barracks were brick-built and provided little protection against bullets and anti-tank rockets alike, and although the paratroopers were heavily outnumbered, in the main the defenders either took shelter deeper in the barracks or in some cases fled from side windows.

A single guard squad had been in the headquarters and it opened fire on the attackers, killing two. In response, Vostrotin's first platoon turned and riddled the building with bullets and HEAT rounds from the BMD's guns, even though this was at point blank range, and the shells' rocket boosters had scarcely had time to cut in. (The PG-15 shells were fired by a small powder charge, then accelerated by a rocket once they had travelled up to 20m.) Those were the only fatalities BG5 would suffer, as they kept the battalion bottled up for the next few hours. It helped that the paratroopers had night vision gear while the Afghans had nothing comparable. An attempt was made by some DRA tanks to relieve them, but after two were destroyed by a couple of 9K111 *Fagot* ATGM (Anti-Tank Guided Missile) launchers from BG7, the sortie was called off. By the time dawn broke at around 6:30am, there had been almost no fighting for hours and, recognizing the situation on the ground, the 2nd Battalion surrendered.

Meanwhile, BG4 had headed to do a similar job on 1st Security Battalion and the Tank Battalion. Given the scale of the task, the Muslim Battalion company under Captain Kudratov committed to the mission was strengthened with a ZSU-23-4 and also two paratrooper *Fagot* ATGM teams in UAZ-469 utility jeeps and fire support from two AGS-17 grenade launchers from BG12. Again, even allowing for their fire support there was an obvious imbalance of numbers: 110 *Spetsnaz* in BTR-60PBs against 700 DRA troops, including 30 T-62 tanks. However, the Soviet advisers had done their job ensuring that most of the tanks were inoperable, removing their batteries in advance and even slipping out components of their pintle-mounted HMGs. The AGS-17s were especially useful in preventing the soldiers from leaving their barracks to get to their vehicles. One crew did manage to brave the hail of fire and start up one of the tanks, but two *Fagot* missiles promptly destroyed it. Again, surprise, professionalism and firepower won the day and these units did not even last the night: some 55 were killed, 250 were captured, and the rest fled.

Phase four

The sequencing of the attack was a delicate one. First, BG1 was meant to take out the emplaced tanks, then swing towards the 3rd Security Battalion. Then, the assault on the Tajbeg Palace would begin. Next came the assault,

almost simultaneously, on the barracks south of the palace and, shortly thereafter, on the north, as well as the anti-air batteries.

Given that BG1's initial plan – simply to bypass the barracks of the 3rd Security Battalion on their way to tackling the dug-in tanks – had not worked out and they had been forced simultaneously to engage the tanks and the defending troops, it became all the more essential that BG6, which was tasked with suppressing the barracks, enter the fray. This was especially the case given that it was also reinforced with two of the handy AGS-17 grenade launcher teams. Once the shooting started, BG6's commander, Senior Lieutenant Kurbandurdy Amangeldyev, ordered his two Muslim Battalion platoons to abandon any attempts at stealth and move at their best speed. One of their BTR-60PBs promptly stalled and there was a hurried reshuffling with BG10, that was moving along the same axis of advance towards the adjacent barracks of the Construction Regiment.

It was just as well that Senior Lieutenant Amangeldyev had opted for speed, as by the time they arrived, the Afghan deputy commander had managed to muster the 3rd Battalion and weapons were being passed around as quickly as they could manage. Under covering fire from the windows of the barracks, some were aggressively moving to take up positions outside it with the clear aim of outflanking the relative handful of Soviets. Equally dangerously, they were trying to set up a PK machine gun on the barracks roof.

One *Grom* commando was already dead, and the handful who remained were hunkered down around their BTRs, their designated fire support (one ZSU-23-4 and two AGS-17s) too busy ensuring the dug-in tanks were destroyed to be able to provide them with any assistance. With the defenders' attention focused on Sakhatov's team on one side of the barracks, though, BG6 was able to deploy on the other and launch the second surprise attack on the 3rd Battalion in 15 minutes.

A volley of rifle and machine-gun fire, along with the 14.5mm rounds of the BTRs' KPVT guns and several RPG-7 and RPG-18 rockets slammed into the barracks building. A number of the Afghans were killed but much more serious was the impact on their morale, especially as their acting commander was rendered unconscious by the blast of a grenade triggered by an incoming round. At this point many soldiers, who had responded with commendable speed and decision at the time of the first attack, as quickly lost their nerve. A couple of them escaped the scene through a side door of the barracks, and this triggered a wider flight. Ironically, what prevented this from being a wholesale rout was the parallel operation by BG10 to blockade the Construction Battalion, as this cut off one of the main lines of retreat. The morale of the 3rd Battalion was broken, though, and although some would resist for another half hour, by the time news spread that the palace had fallen, they were ready to surrender.

The adjacent Construction Battalion was a relatively low-priority target given that it was essentially a conscript non-combat unit largely involved in grounds maintenance, many of whose officers routinely opted to spend their evenings in the city, even when notionally on duty. Nonetheless, given that the barracks did possess an armoury (with a few AK-47 assault rifles but mainly older, but still dangerous, 7.62mm SKS carbines), the 400 soldiers of the unit needed to be neutralized along with the rest of the defenders. Nonetheless, only two *Spetsnaz* platoons were assigned to the task, with BG10 comprising 57 men in 6 BTR-60PBs. However, given that one of the company's APCs suffered a malfunction on the approach, there was a hurried exchange of missions. The 2nd Platoon of the Muslim Battalion's 2nd Company, originally intended to take part in the attack on the 3rd Battalion, was swapped with the 1st Platoon – from whence came the recalcitrant personnel carrier – and entrusted with this task.

Although it was disconcerting to have their mission changed at the eleventh hour and fifty-ninth minute, *Spetsnaz* are meant to be adaptable, and fortunately for them, their phase of the operation went off without a hitch. One BTR-60 and its squad took up positions at each of the barracks' two main entrances, which were at opposite ends of the building, while a third stopped off to one side, to be able to rake its rear (where there was a service entrance to the kitchens). Resistance was minimal: between this unit and the 3rd Battalion some 200 Afghan soldiers ended up surrendering, with the unfortunate Dmitry Volkov, killed in the first exchange of fire, the attackers' only fatality.

Taking out the AAA

The last separate component of Storm-333 was the seizure or destruction of the air defence regiment sited on a hill to the north-west of the palace. While primarily intended to sweep the skies – the *mujahideen* had no air assets, but Amin feared a plot from within his own air force – its rapid-fire guns and heavy machine guns could command the palace and much of the approaches to it, and provide fire support for the defenders the way the Soviets were using their ZSU-23-4s. The 12 KS-19 100mm guns could fire 15 rounds per minute, and their AP-T (Armour Piercing-Tracer) rounds would have no trouble penetrating the armour of the Soviets' various personnel carriers. Likewise, the ZPU-2 twin-mounts could throw a maximum of 1,200 14.5mm rounds per minute out to 3,000m, allowing them to command the battlefield. In addition, the unit possessed powerful spotlights, which might be employed to blind or illuminate attackers, and also an R-142 radio complex on a GAZ-66 truck chassis, which could summon reinforcements. In total, this regiment had an establishment strength of some 400 officers and men, although as was often the case with DRA, there were gaps in the order of battle and also many officers would spend the evenings in the city.

A Soviet military convoy snakes its way through the Afghan hills. One of the reasons why the General Staff was opposed to the invasion was their awareness that this was an environment highly conducive to guerrilla war, and for which the mechanized Red Army was ill-prepared. (Sergei Novikov/ CC 3.0)

In order to take on this force, the Muslim Battalion's Lieutenant Colonel Shvets, an experienced GRU operator, was given a platoon of *Spetsnaz* in four BMPs under Lieutenant Rustam Nazarov to form BG8, along with a separate platoon of fully six AGS-17 automatic grenade launchers. The hope was that after the AA unit had been neutralized, this platoon could use the elevated position they had seized to assist whichever element of the attack most needed it.

The unit arrived just after 7:30pm. The BMPs roared up the hill towards the AA position under cover of suppressive fire from the AGS-17s, whose salvos of VOG-17M 30mm fragmentation grenades were aimed at clearing any gun crews away from their weapons. In the darkness and chaos, one of the BMPs drove into a ditch at the base of the rise: no one was hurt, but the vehicle was impossible to extricate in the midst of the battle. The other three, though, made their way into the middle of the unit, planning to divide the gun positions – which were largely unmanned – from the huts where the gunners were sheltering from the evening cold. Afghan soldiers who had been working on one ZPU-2 tried to bring it to bear on the attackers, but were cut down by fire from the coaxial turret machine guns of two BMPs.

They deployed in such a way as not only to block the Afghans from their guns but also to be able to dissuade any efforts on their part to move towards the palace. In practice, though, none seemed inclined to try it: the DRA troops largely stayed in their huts and the Soviets were too few to go in after them, so while some slipped away into the night, most of the gun crews were still there when dawn broke. At that time, Kolesnik ordered Shvets to disarm the battalion and the Afghans proved perfectly willing to surrender en masse. At the same time, the soldiers from the disabled BMP, who had not dared to abandon their vehicle during the night because of the risk of

mines or being taken for Afghan troops seeking to recapture the guns, were reunited with their comrades. Twelve intact KS-12 guns and all but one of the 16 ZPU-2 mounts were taken, along with around a hundred Afghan soldiers; BG8, by contrast, suffered no casualties.

Inside the palace

By the time the other Soviet combat groups were fully engaged, the remnants of BG2 and BG3 were inside the Tajbeg Palace: fewer than 50 GRU and KGB *Spetsnaz*, most of whom had suffered at least some wounds. They faced more than twice their number of defenders, a mix of uniformed Presidential Security Detachment and *Sarandoy*, Amin's plain-clothes bodyguards, military officers attached to the palace, and some general palace staff willing to fight off this unexpected attack.

Once they had occupied Afghanistan, the Soviets did make real efforts towards a hearts and minds campaign, from building infrastructure to providing medical care. However, the brutality of the initial assault and Amin's fate – to say nothing of subsequent military operations – belies the carefully crafted official image. (Author's Collection)

The ground floor was mainly ceremonial rooms and service facilities, although the communications centre was also here, and some grenades soon ensured that no reinforcements could be summoned. The next struggle was to force a way onto the upper floor, where Amin's offices and private quarters were. This had to be up one of the wide and open staircases, which proved death traps in light of the firepower available to the defenders. Nonetheless, once the attackers had united and had a moment to take a breath and bind their wounds, they concentrated on one staircase. Hand grenades were the obvious option, but also a dangerous one when thrown upwards, as they could easily fall back down and detonate, especially if their arming time was miscalculated. Nonetheless, a PK machine gun was brought up to provide suppressing fire and RGD-5 fragmentation grenades lobbed up towards the top of the stairs and over the banisters of the hall above. The grenades' fuses have a 3–4-second delay, and so the soldiers had to hold on to them for a second or two before throwing them, to minimize the risk of them falling or being kicked back down, which was an unwelcome extra moment

Inside the palace

The Soviet commanders had expected the assault to be as bloody inside the palace as outside it, and they were right. Some Afghans fled or surrendered, but more put up a fierce resistance, even if often outgunned. Here, a collection of Amin loyalists are putting up a last-ditch defence of one of the main stairwells. A plain-clothes officer from Amin's personal protection detail – evident from his use of a German-made Heckler & Koch MP5 submachine gun, exclusively reserved for them – has just shot one attacker. With his colleagues, including a soldier of the 37th Commando Brigade in their distinctive camouflage, being armed only with PM pistols and a single SKS rifle in the hands of a *Sarandoy* security trooper, though, they will not be able to hold back the main force from 3BG, especially as one of the Moslem Battalion soldiers is bringing up a PKM machine gun. The banner is the short-lived *Khalq* flag, that was replaced with a national one the following year, and the dead man on the stairs was a *Khalq* official, evident from the party pin on his lapel.

Soviet soldiers survey the Tajbeg Palace, the morning after the assault. The extensive damage to the building is evident, especially from the bombardment and subsequent fires. (Andrei Abrakov/CC 4.0)

of stress. Indeed one, thrown by *Grom* operator Sergei Golov, rolled back down – he hurriedly threw another and took cover, and fortunately avoided being caught in the blast. They managed to kill or stun the defenders for long enough to allow the quickest Soviets to get up the stairs and secure a beachhead on the upper floor.

By this time there were only eight KGB *Spetsnaz* still fully mobile; Romanov had to stay on the ground floor, having received a severe concussion from a grenade. What followed was a quick and dirty exercise in clearing a building, with the attackers going room-to-room, often hurling grenades in before bursting through the door. After all, the aim was to find and kill Amin, and collateral damage was a decidedly secondary concern. Some of the defenders continued to put up a tough fight, especially Amin's personal bodyguards, *Khalq* loyalists notable for their use of German Heckler & Koch MP5 submachine guns; they were almost the only Afghans to wield these weapons. However, for most of the Afghans, the Soviets' success in forcing their way to the upper floor, combined with the continued thunder of 23mm ZSU rounds on the outer wall, was enough to encourage them to surrender. Several of the commando officers in particular had studied at the Soviet airborne school in Ryazan, and learned not just Russian but Russian soldiers' *mat*, expletive-laden slang, and they used this to appeal to be allowed to surrender.

Before he died, Boyarinov had issued the orders 'don't take prisoners. No one should be left alive.' However, while they certainly were not going to go out of their way to take captives, by this time the exhausted attackers were not about to massacre people indiscriminately. Unable to waste men guarding prisoners and unwilling to lose the momentum of their assault, the *Spetsnaz* simply told them to disarm themselves and head downstairs and surrender again to the first Soviet soldier they saw – most duly did.

When the shooting had first started, the Soviet doctors Alekseyev and Kuznechenkov had initially assumed that it was the *mujahideen* or a counter-coup by Taraki's supporters. They saw Amin in the corridor in a state of confusion and disarray, in shorts and a t-shirt. He was carrying the two bottles of his intravenous drip, with the needles still in his arms. Alekseyev took these out of his arms and applied plasters, and the two doctors helped him into a room that was used as a bar, where he was joined by one of his aides.

By this time, the *Spetsnaz* had reached the upper floor and the doctors heard that they were shouting in Russian. Suspecting what had happened, they took shelter, as Amin's five-year-old son Khwazak rushed into the room in tears, and clasped his father's legs. Still unaware of the identity of the attackers, Amin ordered his aide to contact the Soviet military advisers for help, saying 'The Soviets will help us.' When his aide told him that the attackers were Soviets, he angrily retorted that this was a lie and threw an ashtray at the offending individual. This seemed to have brought him out of his dazed – and still sedated – self and he turned to the telephone, trying to contact first the Chief of General Staff and then the commander of the 4th Tank Brigade. However, all the lines were down thanks to the earlier sabotage, and his energy seemed to dissipate as quickly as it had returned. He numbly admitted, 'I suppose you're right.'

The attackers were nearing, the crack of gunfire and grenades getting louder and louder as they worked their way along the main corridor of the wing of the palace containing Amin's personal quarters. His wife Patmanah began calling for him, and *Zenit* commando Nuritdin Kurbanov – the only remaining member of the assault team who spoke Dari (the Afghan form of Farsi Persian) – translated for Semyonov as she was seized and bound. Unwittingly, though, she had indicated where her husband was, so the *Spetsnaz* headed there. A single bodyguard remained, but he was cut down with a burst of fire. Several stray rounds came through the door and the unfortunate Dr Kuznechenkov was mortally wounded by his own compatriots.

Amin offered no resistance as four *Spetsnaz* burst in; indeed, he seems to have lapsed back into a semi-comatose state from shock or the remaining effects of the poison. At this point, the official accounts become vague, and different versions of the next few minutes have appeared in various articles and books. However, the account that seems to have most currency is that once Amin was identified from a photograph that the assault team had been issued (or else, according to others, by Sayed Gulyabzoy, one of the Afghans supporting the coup), he was simply executed there and then. The deed was done either by a *Grom* commando, or by Gulyabzoy, whether as part of a deliberate ploy to support the cover story, that it was an internal

Afghan affair, or out of simple vengeance. In any case, Amin's corpse was then wrapped in a carpet for the sake of both discretion and also to make it more easily moved.

Mopping up

From the start of the attack on the palace, this had taken just 43 minutes. Maintaining operational security to the last, a radio message to Colonel Kolesnik simply confirmed that 'the primary objective has been achieved'. Until then, the command post had been waiting on a rise next to two ZSU-23-4s, but it now moved to the palace, along with the medical team. Karpukhin, one of the *Grom* team leaders who had taken part in the final assault on the upper floor of the palace, greeted Kolesnik with a smile, showing him his helmet, with a spent bullet lodged in its liner.

Major Kholbayev took charge of establishing a secure perimeter around the palace and extinguishing the fires that had been started by the attack, using the remainder of the Muslim Battalion's 3rd Company. Lieutenant Abdullayev, the company's political officer, did what he could to deploy the personnel carriers which had taken part in storming the palace in a defensive ring, but of the seven, two were burned out, two more disabled, and the turret of a fifth was so damaged that its weapons were inoperable. Fortunately, they would face no further attacks that night.

Emergency medical care was provided to the worst-hurt victims on both sides. Both Amin's sons, 5-year-old Khwazak and 11-year-old Abdur, had been killed in the crossfire or by grenade shrapnel. His daughter Ghaurgati had also been hurt, hit in the leg, but a *Spetsnaz* operator had provided first aid at the time, and Dr Alekseyev then took over her treatment. She and Patmanah would survive. Wounded Afghans were sent off to their own military hospital, in the care of some of the soldiers who had surrendered. The Soviets evacuated their casualties in a convoy to their own embassy clinic. On the way, they were mistaken for DRA reinforcements by paratroopers from the Soviet 103rd Airborne Division involved in securing the Army HQ, and initially fired on. The confusion was quickly dispelled by an especially expletive-laden radio message, and fortunately no one was hurt further in the brief exchange.

When the Soviet commandos involved in the operation had originally been briefed, they had been told that Amin was an agent of the CIA. This was treated with considerable scepticism by operators used to working in the shadow world of *maskirovka*, some of whom commented that in this case he would have been inviting in US, not Soviet troops. Nonetheless, they were professionals, and it did not occur to any to refuse their orders. However, it did mean that as soon as they could, officers from *Zenit*, soon joined by more technical specialists from the embassy's KGB contingent, began to comb through documents at the palace in the hope of finding incriminating evidence. (They found nothing to prove this mythical allegiance.)

Meanwhile, Captain Sakhatov led ten *Spetsnaz* towards the nearby barracks of the Presidential Security Detachment, which had only been

blockaded by BG9, not taken. Together with the paratroopers, they worked through the building; only 12 Afghans remained, and they were taken prisoner. As he led the prisoners out, Sakhatov was fired on and wounded by an unknown assailant. After all, at this point, the Tajbeg compound was a confused mess of flickering flames, individuals who might be stragglers, deserters, or armed DRA hold-outs, and moans, sirens and sporadic gunfire in the night. Some of the defenders, especially from the 3rd Security Battalion, would eventually slip into the mountains beyond the city limits and take up arms against the government. It was a mess. But the mission had been accomplished.

Soviet forces take up positions in front of the Darulaman ('Abode of Peace') Palace in Kabul on 28 November, the DRA's ironic choice for its Defence Ministry, which was seized the night before along with other key buildings. (Henri Bureau/Corbis/VCG via Getty Images)

Death of Amin

The Soviets had no plans to take Amin prisoner. Debilitated by his attempted poisoning, he missed the opportunity to flee from the palace when the assault started, unwilling to believe the Soviets had turned against him. Here, still showing the signs of the IV drip on which he was placed to purge the poisons, he is executed by soldiers of the 2nd Combat Group, one firing a burst into his back after a warrant officer from *Grom* confirmed Amin's identity from a photo he carried for this purpose. The shooter carries a folding-stock AKMS-47 and the soldier guarding the door an AKM-47, dated by the standards of Soviet *Spetsnaz*, but carried to blend in with the Afghan soldiers they were imitating. The white armbands they wore were precisely to identify members of the attacking force. The latter also wears the bulky 6B1 armoured vest, first issued in 1957, but worn by many of the assault team as the best available to them at the time. The *Grom* operator is wearing the uniform of a *Sarandoy* security trooper (note the red collar tabs) and carries an APS Stechkin machine pistol, with its distinctive long, rigid holster, which could be used as a stock. On the floor sprawls the unfortunate Col. Dr Viktor Kuznechenkov, a Soviet military physician assigned to Amin's staff, who had not been warned of the attack, and who was accidentally killed in the crossfire.

ANALYSIS

Poor iron won't make a sharp sword.

Afghan proverb

The Soviet special forces took on almost five times their number of Afghans, and largely elite troops at that, in a mission that many of them had thought was near-suicidal, but their butcher's bill was astonishingly light. They suffered just nine deaths, including Boyarinov, and 69 seriously wounded. (Some accounts put the tally at 14 dead, because they include five killed in a 'friendly fire' incident the next morning.) The Afghan forces lost an estimated 200 dead, and figures for how many were captured that night or morning vary wildly, from 200 to 1,700. This confusion is probably down to the fact that, especially in the earlier stage of Storm-333, the Soviets were not seeking to take prisoners. They could not allow the defenders to reinforce the palace or to withdraw in good order, especially with their heavy weapons. However, their mission was to take the palace and remove Amin; so long as defenders were fleeing the other way, then the outnumbered Soviets were generally happy to let them go. A 'catch and release' policy was thus often informally applied, with Afghans who surrendered being forced to abandon their weapons but then being let go, with a clear warning that if they did anything but flee, next time they would be less lucky.

After Amin's death, Lieutenant Colonel Shvets was made responsible for dealing with the regular prisoners. Officers and non-commissioned officers were separated from the rank-and-file, and kept in a hollow, under guard. As soon as possible, though, he set up a field kitchen to supply tea and basic rations. As he later noted, 'we treated them with humanity, so as not to provoke a mass exodus on their part. Otherwise, if they united and resisted, they could have crushed us with their bare hands.'

Besides, in the midst of the operation, it only made sense to detail soldiers to guard captives in the case of some higher-value prisoners, such as Major Jandar. Even then, this was largely a duty assigned to soldiers too badly

SOVIET CASUALTIES

Captain Dmitri Vasilyevich Volkov, KGB *Grom* (1st BG) attacking DRA tanks

Colonel Grigory Ivanovich Boyarinov, KGB KUOS (2nd BG), in the storming of the palace

Captain Gennady Yegorovich Zudin, KGB *Grom* (2nd BG), in the storming of the palace

Senior Lieutenant Andrei Aleksandrovich Yakushev, KGB Department S (2nd BG), in the storming of the palace

Private Shokirzhon Sultanovich Suleymanov, GRU Muslim Battalion (2nd BG), in the storming of the palace

Sergeant Mirkasym Abdrashimovich Shcherbekov, GRU Muslim Battalion (2nd BG), in the storming of the palace

Senior Lieutenant Boris Aleksandrovich Suvorov, KGB *Zenit* (3rd BG), in the storming of the palace

Corporal Amangeldy Shampitovich Kalmagombetov, 9th Company, 345th Independent Guards Airborne Regiment (5th BG), attacking the 2nd Security Battalion

Private Vladimir Vasilyevich Savoskin, 9th Company, 345th Independent Guards Airborne Regiment (5th BG), attacking the 2nd Security Battalion

Another five soldiers of the Muslim Battalion were killed the next day by Soviet paratroopers in a 'friendly fire' incident.

wounded for more mobile missions. While the politically significant figures like the survivors of Amin's family were then handed over to the new DRA regime and sent to Pul-i-Charkhi, most of the rank-and-file prisoners were later released and returned to the DRA military that was now commanded by Karmal's new government. Amin's body was buried that night in an unmarked site on the palace grounds, along with those of both of his sons, close to the mass grave in which the other fallen defenders were laid.

Taking Kabul

Meanwhile, Kabul had fallen to the Soviets. As the assault began, the 345th Air Assault Regiment supported by elements of the 317th and 350th Regiments of the 103rd Guards Air Assault Division had moved out of their base at Bagram. They soon came under fire from an Afghan anti-air battery outside the airbase, cranking their 85mm M1939 (52-K) guns down for direct fire, but the paratroopers promptly took the offensive, seizing their positions at the cost of just a single man injured. It helped that, once again, Soviet military advisers and technicians had been playing gremlin that day, removing components from some guns and secretly replacing locks on ammunition stores with new ones to which they had the only keys. Even so, speed was the paratroopers' best weapon; they sent the Afghan soldiers running, left a single squad to secure the guns, and carried on into the city in a mix of BMDs, GAZ-66 jeeps and Zil-131 trucks.

As one of the soldiers reminisced: 'Kabul met us with "fireworks". It wasn't a holiday – there was just gunfire everywhere, and it seemed that the city was on fire.' Nonetheless, a combination of surprise and the efforts made to disrupt communications and the chain of command ensured that Afghan resistance was sporadic and disorganized.

Spearheaded by *Zenit* and *Grom* commando teams, the Soviets quickly seized the Central Communications Centre, Pul-i-Charkhi Prison, the main post office, the General Staff building, the TV and radio centre, the main telegraph office, the Defence and Interior Ministries, and the headquarters of the KAM secret police and the *Sarandoy*. They were successful in every case, despite the forces deployed at each location. As well as its regular prison warders, for example, a full company of *Sarandoy* was guarding Pul-i-Charkhi, and the 15th Tank Brigade was based nearby. Likewise, the TV and radio centre was guarded by four BMPs, four tanks, and four emplaced DShK heavy machine guns, but was taken by the 345th Independent Airborne Regiment's reconnaissance company, reinforced by a ZU-23 anti-aircraft gun squad and nine *Zenit* operators, and accompanied by Mohammad Aslam Watanjar, Taraki's former defence minister. The paratroopers used their BMDs to crash through the building's gates, then RPG-18 *Mukha* rocket launchers to destroy three tanks and a BMP while the *Zenit* commandos entered the building. Watanjar was then able to persuade the remaining defenders to stand down.

The General Staff building was secured with the direct intervention of General Ryabchenko, commander of the 103rd Guards Airborne Division, who brought a *Zenit* team right into the building to meet Afghan Chief of the General Staff General Yakub under the pretext of an introductory

The Soviet expectation had been that, with Amin gone, a reunited PDPA could revive the DRA and defeat the rebels both militarily and in a hearts and minds campaign. Ultimately they failed, but staged photo opportunities such as this welcome given by locals in Khost to DRA troops certainly conveys Moscow's (vain) hopes. (TASS via Getty Images)

A column of armoured vehicles and trucks from the 201st Motor Rifle Division arrives in Kabul on 30 January 1980, as part of a reinforcement of the 108th Division. (Bettmann/Getty Images)

meeting. When the explosion that severed the communications cables sounded, the notoriously suspicious Yakub tried to reach an MP-5 submachine gun he kept in his office and was restrained – not easily, as he was a tall, fit ex-commando – by *Zenit* team leader Major Rozin, who was posing as Ryabchenko's aide.

It was a sign of the sudden and shocking nature of the assault, as well as the preparations and professionalism of the Soviet special forces, that they took only a single casualty, an operator from *Zenit* killed while the Interior Ministry, which was guarded by 350 *Sarandoy*, was being taken by a commando team under Major Yuri Melnik and two VDV platoons. Overall, DRA garrisons around Kabul were also blockaded – some units were willing to be confined to their barracks and wait and see what the outcome would be, but others tried to break out, leading to sporadic firefights, although there was no coherent resistance. In case the DRA troops managed to deploy tanks, for example, as soon as they had seized the main government district – which contained most of these buildings – then the paratroopers' BMDs were dug in to provide a degree of anti-armour defence, along with SPG-9 recoilless rifle and RPG-7V anti-tank grenade launcher teams. That assault never happened, though.

The invasion

On the night of 24 December, the commander of TurkVO, Colonel General Yuri Maximov, had reported to Moscow that the invasion forces were ready. The next day, Minister of Defence Ustinov formally confirmed the start of Baikal-79 for 3pm (Moscow time). The first troops of the 40th Army to cross the border were reconnaissance detachments and an Assault Landing Battalion of the 56th Independent Guards Air Assault Brigade, which secured the critical entry point of the Salang Pass. The 108th Motor Rifle Division under General Konstantin Kuzmin then followed, crossing a pontoon bridge over the Amu Darya. Given that the pretext was that the Soviets were coming to help secure Kabul, the second, western pincer of the Soviet invasion waited until 28 December, when the 5th Motor Rifle Division under General Yuri Shatalin would cross the border from its base in Kushka, moving to Herat and Shindand.

As the land invasion was taking place, the bulk of Major General Ivan Ryabchenko's 103rd Air Assault Division and rest of the 345th Independent Airborne Regiment began to be lifted to Bagram and Kabul airport. Tragically, an Il-76 transport aircraft lost power and crashed into a mountain while nearing Kabul, exploding on impact and killing all seven

crew and 37 paratroopers on board. By 27 December, they were ready to move out and secure the city. The advance guard of the 108th Division had reached north-eastern Kabul by midday on the 28th.

Politics and revenge

On 23 December, Karmal had again been smuggled into Bagram and kept hidden and guarded by officers of the KGB Ninth Directorate and a team of *Alfa* bodyguards. Late on the 27th, after it had been confirmed that Amin was dead, a pre-recorded message was played on Kabul Radio, saying that 'today the torture machine of Amin has been smashed' and vowing a new age and a new PDPA again uniting *Khalq* and *Parcham*. Karmal himself was taken in a column of armoured personnel carriers into Kabul on the morning of the 28th to take up his new position, courtesy of Moscow, just in time for the arrival of the 'soldier-internationalists' of the 108th.

Reflecting the official line that this had essentially been an internal affair between Afghans, the official announcement of Amin's death read that he had been 'sentenced to death at a revolutionary trial for crimes against the state and the sentence had been carried out'. Gulyabzoy and Watanjar would later confirm his death (if it is true that Gulyabzoy had actually pulled the

Soviet paratroopers from the 103rd Guards Airborne Division on patrol in the streets of Kabul immediately after their seizure of the city. As was usual in anything other than combat operations, the crewmen are not 'buttoned up' inside their BMDs' cramped hulls. (François LOCHON/ Gamma-Rapho via Getty Images)

The Soviet invasion

Storm-333 was just the first phase of the Soviet invasion of Afghanistan. Here, elements of the 108th Motor Rifle Division proceed down the road to Kabul, waved on by a 'Regulator' – or traffic controller – from the Commandant's Service military police. A line of BTR-60PB personnel carriers are parked along the verge behind a ZIL-131 radio truck as BMP-1 infantry combat vehicles and a T-62 tank move to the front. Despite the cold, several soldiers are riding on top of the BMP-1, both because of mistrust of its thin armour protection and also because of the cramped conditions inside; during longer trips, soldiers often took turns on top to allow those inside more space. Given that the DRA forces had also been equipped with T-62 tanks, this has also been painted with white 'invasion stripes' for recognition purposes. Although the invasion was unopposed, a Mi-24 Hind-D helicopter gunship provides top cover, just in case.

trigger, then one might suppose he was in a good place to do this). Several of Amin's closest supporters were indeed subjected to a quick farce of a 'trial' and then a bullet in the back of the neck in the very same Pul-i-Charkhi prison to which they had condemned so many of their enemies.

There was meant to be, though, no indiscriminate bloodletting. The Soviets, it is worth remembering, wanted to preserve as much of the PDPA and the DRA state apparatus as possible. This was to be a new start, with *Parcham* and *Khalq* working together to defeat the rebellion and build a new socialist Afghanistan together now that the murderous Amin was gone. If only it was to prove that easy, not least because Karmal now turned on his former persecutors, locking up or executing *Khalqi* officials, just as they had treated *Parchamis*. In vain, Moscow tried to counsel a more conciliatory approach, and the seeds of future PDPA division and dissent were sown.

A textbook start to a misconceived war

Given the secretive nature of the operation – and the KGB's reluctance to admit what had happened to him – Colonel Boyarinov's fate only emerged during the glasnost campaigns of the later Gorbachev era, when the Communist Party was relaxing censorship. He retrospectively became hailed as one of the fathers of the modern special forces. (Author's Collection)

After all, this was not just a textbook operation, it was in many ways a metaphor for much of the Soviet way of war: meticulously planned, ruthlessly applied, but subject to problems as soon as events deviated from the plan. Even during the preparations, much seemed to be being organized at the last minute and on the sketchiest information. Kolesnik only received detailed plans for the palace, for example, the day before the operation, and Vostrotin's paratroopers were expected to use the compound's roads but had not been given basic information about their quality and width. The fear of BMDs shedding tracks by driving at high speed over potholed asphalt was a real one, for example, when the loss of a single vehicle would have a significant impact on a team's total firepower. Official accounts tend to emphasize the complex, interconnected planning, which was certainly in evidence. Tales by the participants, though, also highlight the last-minute improvisations and the errors made. Both perspectives are valid.

Kolesnik himself later admitted that 'the operation to seize the Palace seemed unthinkable'. Nonetheless, thanks to some often inspired 'diversionary operations' around Kabul and the skill and courage of the KGB and GRU *Spetsnaz*, the unthinkable was achieved. This turned what could have been a bloody, contested Soviet occupation of Afghanistan's towns and cities into a near-bloodless fait accompli, and allowed most of the DRA's armed and security forces to be brought into the new Karmal regime. That invasion had also been carefully planned, with each bridge across which the Soviets had to roll their tanks and trucks already surveyed for the weight it could take, each tunnel measured, fuel stores in place and ammunition supplies prepared. By the morning of the 28th, Soviet military police were directing traffic on Kabul's main intersections while their Afghan counterparts were being briefed on the new realities, and news anchors were being presented with pre-written texts to read on air.

So far, so smooth. However, even during Storm-333 a tendency towards trouble emerging when things started to deviate from the plan became clear as events began to acquire their own momentum. Friendly fire proved as much a danger as the defenders – as Colonel Boyarinov could attest – and continued to be a challenge, even after the chaos of the initial assault. On 28 December, for example, a detachment of the Muslim Battalion's 3rd Company was deployed to seize the headquarters of the DRA's 1st Corps. A company of the 103rd Guards Airborne Division that was also involved in the attack fired on them, under the misapprehension that they were DRA reinforcements, given their uniforms. Five of the *Spetsnaz* died in a hail of fire from the paratroopers' BMDs before Senior Lieutenant Abdullayev could get close enough to hail his compatriots: more members of the Muslim Battalion than had fallen the night before, taking the Tajbeg.

That same evening, another incident almost claimed the lives of all the leading lights of Storm-333: Kolesnik, Drozdov, Shvets, Kozlov and Semyonov. Followed by Khalbayev in a BTR, they were driving back to the Muslim Battalion in a captured government Mercedes, and although they had already agreed recognition challenges and responses with Lieutenant General Guskov, who was commanding the VDV contingent in Kabul, they were hastily fired on by jumpy paratroopers near the General Staff building. The car stalled, and its occupants hurriedly (and apparently rather profanely) called out to the paratroopers and established their bona fides. When they got out, though, they discovered five bullet holes in the car. The rounds had fortunately buried themselves in the engine block. As Drozdov recalled, 'a little higher and everyone would have died'. He added, seemingly more aggrieved by the fact that it would have been such a stupid death as anything else, 'so ineptly'. At the time, he sarcastically congratulated the lieutenant in charge of the paratroopers 'thank you for not teaching them to shoot straight'.

Second, it would become clear how far the Soviets had miscalculated the mood of the country and the Afghans' resistance to foreign domination, however much it may be presented as 'fraternal assistance'. An early harbinger of this was the mutiny of the DRA's 4th Artillery Regiment in Baghlan province. In January 1980, they rose against the government and a motor rifle battalion of the Soviet 186th Regiment, reinforced by a tank company, an artillery battery and an extra mechanized infantry company, was deployed from Kunduz to suppress them. As this task force approached the township of Nakhrin, it was attacked by *mujahideen* on horseback, who had to be dispersed by helicopter gunships. The Soviets pushed through, encircled the 4th Regiment and forced it to surrender, losing only two dead in the process, but the engagement highlighted some serious problems for

As it became clear that the invasion would not be a short, demonstrative operation but a drawn-out counter-insurgency war, the Soviets were forced to adopt new tactics, with the *Spetsnaz* and paratroopers often taking the lead. Here, a paratrooper patrol prepares to board an Mi-8 helicopter to be airlifted back to base. (Russian Ministry of Defence/ CC 4.0)

the future: the continuing flow of DRA mutineers to the rebellion, the tacit alliance between them and *mujahideen*, and the constant need for the Soviets to deploy forces out of their bastions in the towns and cities and into the rough countryside where they were subject to ambush and misdirection.

Chief of the General Staff Ogarkov and the other critics and sceptics were, after all, quite right. This was to be no 'quick, victorious little war', not the six-month demonstrative deployment the Kremlin had so glibly assumed.

After the storm

On 10 January, Kolesnik and others from the command team flew from Tashkent back to Moscow with their operational plan and after-action reports. They were taken first to the 'Aquarium', the GRU's headquarters, where they were greeted and congratulated by General Ivashutin himself. Kolesnik was then conveyed to a personal meeting with Defence Minister Ustinov. He hugged the hitherto-unknown Kolesnik and launched into a lengthy and detailed debrief, noting with chagrin and disappointment that Ivanov and Magometov had not signed the operational plan. After an hour and a half's meeting – an unusually long commitment in the minister's crowded schedule – he personally showed Kolesnik out. Witnessing this, Marshal Sokolov, the First Deputy Minister of Defence, said, 'Well, Comrade Colonel, the minister has never escorted any of *us* to the door.'

It was meant in good humour, but it accurately conveyed the appreciation felt in Moscow for the men who had pulled off such a feat. In April 1980, by a secret decree of the Presidium of the Supreme Soviet of the USSR, Boyarinov was posthumously made a Hero of the Soviet Union, the country's highest

Babrak Karmal being welcomed by DRA soldiers in a no-doubt wholly spontaneous and unstaged photo opportunity. (Russian Ministry of Defence/CC 4.0)

honour, along with three survivors: Colonel Kolesnik, Major Karpukhin and Captain Second Rank Kozlov. Kolesnik would go on to be made a major general and head the GRU's special operations directorate. Yuri Drozdov

VALERY VOSTROTIN

The choice of young Senior Lieutenant Valery Alexandrovich Vostrotin to play a key role alongside the KGB and GRU *Spetsnaz* of Storm-333 was no accident, as he had already been identified as one of the rising stars of the VDV. As it was, though, the Afghan War would prove to be the making of this paratrooper, who went on to become a Colonel General, one of today's highest profile *afgantsy*, as the veterans of the war are known.

He was born in 1952 in the industrial Chelyabinsk Region from a working-class family. Like many in his situation, the military proved a way out, and at age 19 he graduated from the Sverdlovsk Suvorov Military School, and joined the VDV right away. He was leading his own paratrooper platoon within four years (and, like any politically savvy young officer with an eye on his career, had joined the Communist Party), then rose steadily such that by 1979 he was a company commander in the 345th Guards Air Assault Regiment of the 105th Guards Air Assault based in Fergana, Uzbekistan. After Storm-333, he continued to serve in the so-called Limited Contingent of Forces in Afghanistan, but in July 1980 was seriously wounded. As soon as he had recovered, he returned to Afghanistan. As further evidence he was being groomed for higher ranks, in 1982 he was enrolled in the M.V. Frunze Military Academy, graduating with honours in 1985. He then went to the 300th Guards Airborne Regiment of the 98th Guards Airborne Division, first as deputy commander, then commander. In 1986, he took command of the 345th Independent Guards Airborne Regiment in Afghanistan, taking part in several key actions including Operation Magistral, lifting the siege of Khost. His unit was one of the last to leave Afghanistan, in February 1989.

By then a colonel, he took command of the 98th Guards Airborne Division. In 1992, he went to the Military Academy of the General Staff of the Armed Forces, graduating in 1994. By this time, the Soviet Union had collapsed and post-Soviet Russia was in chaos. He accepted a position as Deputy Minister for Civil Defence, Emergencies and Disaster Relief, which he held until 2003, when he was elected to the State Duma, the lower house of parliament, as a representative of the nationalist Unity and Fatherland Party bloc. In 2011, he was also elected chair of the Union of Russian Paratroopers veterans' movement.

Colonel General Vostrotin continues to play an active role in veterans' affairs and the new nationalist political agenda. He chairs the Ministry of Defence's Interdepartmental Commission on Prisoners of War and Missing Persons and also the board of trustees of Patriot Park, a military theme park of sorts outside Moscow. His decorations include Hero of the Soviet Union with Gold Star, the Order of the Red Banner, For Merit to the Fatherland, For Courage and For Honour, two Orders of the Red Star, the Impeccable Service Medal and five from the DRA, including the Order of Friendship of Peoples and the Medal 'To a Warrior-Internationalist from the Grateful Afghan People'.

Валерий
ВОСТРОТИН

Прости, не смогли мы от горя сберечь
Твой ласковый взор и твоих хрупких плеч.
Ты сильная, мама, и выстоишь ты,
За все остальное с отцом нас прости.

Прости, по-другому мы жить не могли
И легкой тропою по свету не шли.
Наш долг нас позвал,
Он позвал нас вперед
По трудной дороге военных невзгод.

Прости, мне себя уберечь не дал бог,
Я жизнью солдатской прикрыться не мог.
Пойми, моя мама, поверь и прости,
Иначе не могут Отчизны сыны.

Валерий Бурков

Valery Vostrotin became quite literally a poster child of the war, as initial attempts to pretend there were no Soviet troops in Afghanistan gave way first to an admission of their presence and then to elevate the 'soldier-internationalists' into propaganda icons. This image is Vostrotin's, from a series of small posters produced to tell the stories of soldiers made Heroes of the Soviet Union. (Author's Collection)

was awarded the Order of the October Revolution, *Grom* commander Major Romanov and Muslim Battalion commander Major Khalbayev the Order of Lenin, and Lieutenant Colonel Shvets, Major Semyonov and Senior Lieutenant Vostrotin the Order of the Red Banner. Some 400 KGB officers involved in Storm-333 or the wider operation were awarded orders and medals of some kind, along with 300 officers and soldiers of the GRU Muslim Battalion. As presumed compensation for his being killed in an operation about which he hadn't been warned, Colonel Dr Kuznechenkov posthumously received the Order of the Red Banner. His colleague Dr Alekseyev had to make do with a Certificate of Honour and getting out of Afghanistan alive.

On 10 January 1980, the Muslim Battalion flew back to Chirchik, but at the end of 1981 it – now known by its proper name of the 154th Special Designation Detachment – returned to Afghanistan as the Soviets began to adapt their forces in light of the fact that this was not going to be a short or easy war. The 154th OSN operated in the north of the country until May 1988, especially storming *mujahideen* bases and intercepting rebel supply convoys, from 1985 being subordinated to the 15th *Spetsnaz* Brigade. When the Soviet Union was dissolved at the end of 1991, the 15th Brigade became part of the armed forces of independent Uzbekistan.

Zenit and *Grom* were likewise soon withdrawn from Afghanistan. For a while, *Zenit* had provided close protection details for Karmal and some other VIPs, but a new detail of officers from the KGB's Ninth Directorate was brought in. *Grom* was reintegrated into the *Alfa* anti-terrorism command, which expanded steadily through the turbulent 1980s. After operations in Afghanistan in 1979–80 under Colonel Polyakov, *Zenit* was reconfigured in July 1980 as *Kaskad* ('Cascade') under Captain Kozlov. It would expand to five separate units with a total strength of around a thousand men, incorporating the Interior Ministry's *Kobalt* special operations team. In 1981, it would also be the basis for *Vympel* ('Pennant'), the *Spetsnaz* unit of the KGB's First Chief Directorate's Department S, intended for covert operations – in war or peace – abroad.

Zenit became *Kaskad* and in due course *Vympel* ('Pennant'), an anti-terrorist commando team that in the 1990s would specialize in securing nuclear facilities. (Troncospetsnaz/CC-SA 4.0)

As for the 9th Company, that would go on to become one of the most famous units of the Afghan War, known for tough soldiering and an unusual degree of initiative. Admittedly, that was after a rocky beginning, being upbraided by their divisional commander for looting in the chaos of post-invasion Kabul. To an extent, this was perhaps the flipside of their swashbuckling style, one that seems to have become ingrained in the unit culture and survived the regular ebb and flow of new cohorts of fresh conscripts. The company fought throughout the Afghan War, in operations from interdictions of rebel supply caravans to rescues of captured soldiers. It acquired a particular reputation for tenacity when, in January 1988, it held Hill 3234, a height commanding the strategic Gardez to Khost road, against 12 fierce attacks by some 250 *mujahideen* over a period of a day and a half. They suffered six fatalities, and inflicted up to 200 casualties on the rebels, some of whom may have actually been Pakistani special forces. A fictionalized version of this incident was made into a blockbusting Russian film, *Ninth Company*.

Having refused to put pen to paper in support of Kolesnik's plan beforehand – presumably out of both wounded pride and also a belief that it would fail – both Chief Military Adviser Magometov and KGB *rezident* Ivanov subsequently tried to get him to allow them to sign it after the event. He refused. Ivanov's field career ended soon thereafter and he became a foreign policy adviser back in Moscow. Magometov, in fairness, was considered to have performed a valuable service in scotching Ivanov's half-baked initial operation and also to have done a first-rate job of managing the logistical support for the invasion. In August 1980, he was wounded and transferred back to the USSR and made first deputy head of the Frunze Military Academy and later maintained close contacts with the veterans' movement. Indeed, he died after a heart attack in August 1989, while giving a speech at a rally of *afgantsy*.

CONCLUSION

One who runs will also fall.
Afghan proverb

Storm-333 is still being interpreted and reinterpreted by Russians today to learn lessons, but also make points. The Soviet war in Afghanistan is a painful and difficult historical experience for today's Russia, after all. On the one hand, it can claim not to have anything to do with the actions of a different regime, of a different state. That this was a *Soviet* blunder, not a *Russian* one. On the other, Vladimir Putin has clearly embarked on an attempt to cherry-pick the elements of Soviet and even Tsarist history that best fit his message that Russia is a country with unique strengths and a singular global mission. The Soviets did not really lose the Afghan War: they could have continued to sustain their commitment there, but withdrew because reformist leader Mikhail Gorbachev saw no advantage in doing so and a clear political gain from leaving. However, they certainly failed to win it. No amount of spin can change this, so instead the focus has shifted to specific elements of the war that do fit Putin's patriotic message more neatly.

Storm-333 is clearly one such episode, able to be presented as a relatively neat surgical strike, a daring blow by a handful of Soviet commandos, a triumph of both planning and battlefield skills. As a result, there is a plethora of books and articles about the operation, which in fairness do not omit the tragedies and the blunders, but certainly emphasize the drama and the victory.

A typical view, in this case from an online magazine for fans of Russian military history, is that it was an operation 'unparalleled in the history of the world's special services' and 'one of the brightest pages in the history of the KUOS'. Indeed, although these are absent from professional studies and more serious histories, the notion that Amin was a CIA agent has become orthodoxy for many. There is even a whole apocryphal history of what would have happened had he not been neutralized, including a massive landing of American troops at Kandahar, Afghanistan's second city, and the deployment

of nuclear Pershing missiles and an electronic intelligence-gathering facility on the Soviet border. This is, though, wholly mythical.

As the end of 2019 led to inevitably '40 years after' retrospectives, some parallels were drawn with what is regarded as another triumph of Russian special forces: the near-bloodless seizure of Crimea. In the popular press, this simply becomes an opportunity for lauding Russian martial skills, but professional studies are less breathless and more critical. Storm-333 has long been studied as a testcase in *Spetsnaz* operations for its technical lessons, especially in the General V. F. Margelov Ryazan Guards Higher Airborne Twice Red Banner Order of Suvorov Command School, the VDV officer training academy, the Military Academy of the General Staff and the Academy of the Federal Security Service.

The overall tenor has been to praise the operation as a resounding success, but also to stress that it depended not only on the initiative and professionalism of the commandos but detailed and comprehensive planning and a use of all means to maximize its chances, including sabotage by KGB agents, disinformation and subversion, as well as seamless integration of KGB, GRU and VDV forces. This was likewise evident during the 40-year retrospectives, and is worth highlighting precisely because it has become a central tenet of modern Russian *spetsoperatsii*, special operations. Much

The memorial to the fallen in the Great Patriotic War, Afghanistan and the fighting in August–September 1999 against jihadist rebels in the Botlikh region. (Russian Presidential Administration/ CC 4.0)

The monument in Victory Park in Moscow to the Soviet 'soldier-internationalists' who fell in Afghanistan and other imperial wars of the time. (Author's Collection)

of the Western hype about so-called 'hybrid warfare' focuses on the way that in Crimea, in south-eastern Ukraine, and to a lesser degree in Syria, the Russians put a great premium on integrating not just typical combined-arms military capabilities but also covert operations, information warfare and suborned locals. This is a warfighting tradition that predates Storm-333, but nonetheless that particular operation continues to be cited as a prime example of how well it could work in the twentieth century, and will no doubt continue to inform Russian operations in the twenty-first.

FURTHER READING

Belyaev, Eduard, *Musulmanskii batal'on* (Eksmo, 2012)

Braithwaite, Rodric, *Afgantsy: The Russians in Afghanistan, 1979–89* (Profile, 2011)

Drozdov, Yuri, *Zapiski nachal'nika nelegal'noy razvedki* (Russkii Biograficheskiy Institut, 1999)

Feifer, Gregory, *The Great Gamble. The Soviet War in Afghanistan* (HarperCollins, 2009)

Fremont-Barnes, Gregory, *The Soviet–Afghan War 1979–89* (Osprey, 2012)

Galeotti, Mark, *Afghanistan: The Soviet Union's Last War* (Frank Cass/Routledge, 1995)

Galeotti, Mark, *Spetsnaz: Russia's Special Forces* (Osprey, 2015)

Liakhovsky, Alexander, *Tragediya i Doblest Afgana* (Iskona, 1995)

Liakhovsky, Alexander, *Inside the Soviet Invasion of Afghanistan and the Seizure of Kabul, December 1979* (Woodrow Wilson Center Cold War International History Project Working Paper, 2007)

Murin, Valerii & Vladimir Surodin, *Spetsnaz Rossii. Istoriya i Sovremennost'* (Granitsa, 2017)

Runov, Valentin, *Afganskaya Voina. Boyevye operatsii* (Eksmo, 2010)

Skrynnikov, Mikhail, *Spetsnaz VDV. Diversionno-razvedyvatel'nye operatsii v Afgane* (Yauza, 2005)

Sukholesskii, AV, *Spetsnaz GRU v Afganistane 1979–1989* (Russkaya Panorama, 2012)

Urban, Mark, *War in Afghanistan, 2nd edition* (Macmillan, 1990)

INDEX